On Liturgical Theology

Aidan Kavanagh

On Liturgical Theology

The Hale Memorial Lectures of
Seabury-Western Theological Seminary,
1981

Pueblo Publishing Company

New York

Design: Frank Kacmarcik

Scriptural pericopes from the Revised Standard Version.

Copyright © 1984 Pueblo Publishing Co., Inc.
1860 Broadway, New York, N.Y. 10023. All rights reserved.

ISBN: 0–916134–67–9
Printed in the United States of America.

In memory of
Alexander Schmemann

Contents

ut legem credendi lex statuat supplicandi

Prosper of Aquitaine[1]

Preface

This book began as two sets of lectures on themes which have become increasingly related in my own thought. The earlier were the MacKinnon Lectures on Church and World given at the Atlantic School of Theology, Halifax, Nova Scotia, in 1980. The later were the Hale Lectures, given on liturgical theology at Seabury-Western Theological Seminary, Evanston, Illinois, in 1982.

Here I have combined the two sets of lectures, recasting both as seemed appropriate to draw them into an even closer relationship than they had when they were composed originally. Although they were written later, the Hale Lectures were much on my mind as the MacKinnon Lectures were in preparation, and both series have occupied me for the past four years. While distinct, they are not separable in conception or intent.

Their union I have entitled, cautiously, *On Liturgical Theology*. This is because I do not wish to suggest that what is contained here is a liturgical theology whole and complete. Even less does it constitute the only possible liturgical theology. The book is in fact only an extended essay in eight main parts concerning something that appears to be part equivocation and part rumor. It is equivocation in that nearly anything theologians write on liturgy is often called liturgical theology, in spite of the fact that such works seem on closer examination to be either dogmatic theologies *about* the liturgy or, more subtly and elegantly, systematic theologies done by giving greater weight to some liturgical data. In the first type, "liturgical" denotes the object of theological effort. In the second type, "liturgical" signals the inclusion of certain data or sources within the effort itself.

In neither instance, however, does the adjective "liturgical" require that the act of performing the liturgy modify, alter, or otherwise affect theological effort; nor that liturgy itself be viewed as a series of acts which constitute theology in the first instance; nor that the peculiar assembly of persons who worship liturgically be regarded as a theological corporation in any but a metaphorical sense, if that. But the very existence of the equivocation contributes to the rumor that there may indeed be something somewhere which is properly *liturgical* theology, although its face is known only in silhouette, its method is elusive, its practitioners nameless, and its results problematic.

The book is meant to do little more than reduce the breadth of equivocation and give some substance to the rumor of liturgical theology's existence. If it succeeds even partially in either task it will be enough. It will not raise every question or solve every problem, and I hope it will avoid slipping into yet another dull disquisition on hermeneutical complications. The book is intended to be an informal and often rhetorical safari in search of theology and liturgy, and an assay of their relationship.

Thanks are due the Atlantic School of Theology and Seabury-Western Theological Seminary for their kindness in requesting the original lectures and for their patience in listening to them. Thanks are also due those who gave the Hale series critical and constructive hearing as I worked to develop them further, namely, the monks of Mount Melleray Abbey in Ireland, the faculty and students of the Yale Institute of Sacred

Music, and the students of liturgy in the Department of Theology of the University of Notre Dame during the summer of 1983. Finally, particular thanks belong to the Hale Endowment and to Pueblo Publishing Company for their willingness to see the book in print, and to the Reverend David Fagerberg for typing the manuscript.

Aidan Kavanagh, O.S.B.
The Divinity School, Yale University
Easter 1984

THE HALE LECTURES OF SEABURY-WESTERN
THEOLOGICAL SEMINARY

1908   Peter C. Lutkin. *Music in the Church* (Mowbray, 1910).

1910   John Wordsworth. *The National Church of Sweden* (Mowbray, 1911).

1913   Anthony Mitchell. *Biographical Studies in Scottish Church History.*

1914   S.A.B. Mercer. *The Ethiopic Liturgy: Its Sources, Development, and Present Form* (Mowbray, 1915).

1922   Frank Gavin. *Some Aspects of Contemporary Greek Orthodox Thought* (Mowbray, 1923).

1928   Frederick C. Grant. *New Horizons of the Christian Faith* (Mowbray, 1928).

1930   Burton Scott Easton. *Christ in the Gospels* (Scribner, 1930).

1932   John Rathbone Oliver. *Pastoral Psychiatry and Mental Health* (Scribner, 1932).

1933   William George Peck. *The Social Implications of the Oxford Movement* (Scribner, 1933).

1935   Winfred Douglas. *Church Music in History and Practice: Studies in the Praise of God* (Scribner, 1937).

1937   Henry St. George Tucker. *The History of the Episcopal Church in Japan* (Scribner, 1938).

1938   Fleming James. *Personalities of the Old Testament* (Scribner, 1939).

1943   E. Clowes Chorley. *Men and Movements in the American Episcopal Church* (Scribner, 1946).

1947   Alec R. Vidler. *Witness to the Light: F.D. Maurice's Message for Today* (Scribner, 1948).

1950   Leonard Hodgson. *The Doctrine of the Atonement* (Scribner, 1951).

1952   Royden Keith Yerkes. *Sacrifice in Greek and Roman Religions and in Early Judaism* (Scribner, 1952).

1953   Powell Mills Dawley. *John Whitgift and the English Reformation* (Scribner, 1954).

1959   Arthur Michael Ramsey. *An Era in Anglican Theology: From Gore to Temple* (Scribner, 1960).

1962   Henry R. McAdoo. *The Spirit of Anglicanism: A Survey of Angelican Theological Method in the Seventeeth Century* (Scribner, 1965).

1963   Eugene Fairweather. *God and His Created Image.*

1966   John Moorman. *The Vatican Council. The Ecumenical Movement and the Anglican Communmion.*

1970   Reginald H. Fuller. *Some Aspects of Pauline Theology.*

1972   David E. Jenkins.

Liturgy and World

Chapter One

Introduction:
Discoursing about Church and World

There are several things the reader should know at the outset about the author's biases as they affect his way of arguing important matters. It is not necessary that the reader share these biases, but it really should be known that they exist and what forms they take. For the author is about to act as a certain sort of critic of the ways in which we have come to hold conventionally certain radical truths, and to live conventionally certain radical social embodiments of these truths—truths and embodiments which really cannot be held or lived conventionally at all.

In this light the reader ought to keep in mind four things about the author as critic.

First, he is the creature of a deeply sacramental tradition of orthodoxy, which means first "right worship" and only secondarily doctrinal accuracy. This is very radical. It implies that worship conceived broadly is what gives rise to theological reflection, rather than the other way around. In Prosper of Aquitaine's phrasing, it is the law of worship which founds or establishes the law of belief—rather as a foundation establishes a house or as the virtue of justice founds the law. The axiom in all three cases is irreversible: it is not law which makes justice possible, not the house which establishes the foundation, not beliefs which enable worship. Furthermore, since this notion of worship is sacramental throughout and makes use of every symbolic analogy available to us as inmates of a created order, the world is included at the very core of what founds or establishes the belief upon which theology reflects. Since Christian worship swims in creation as a fish swims in water, theology has no option but to accept the created world as a necessary component of every equation and conclusion it produces. Christian theology cannot talk of God, any more than Einstein could talk of energy, without including the "mass" of the world squared by the constant of God's eternal will to save in Christ. Einstein's equation is ruthless because it is true. The Christian equation is no less ruthless because it too is true. Neither equation permits tampering. Take mass out of $E = mc^2$ and the result is not the way things are in physics. Take the created world, with all its intractable ambiguities, out of a theological statement and the result is not the way things are in orthodox Christian faith.

Second, the author is a liturgical scholar. This causes him to be more at home in the iconic East than in the pictorial West. Pictures are about meaning. Icons are about being. This difference shows in the contrasts between eastern and western Christian worship. The latter tends to exploit meaning in such raw and aggressive quantity that congregations often are reduced to passivity, seated in pews with texts before them in order to give their full attention to the meaning purveyed in the service. Eastern worship, on the other hand, tends to be less cerebral and more open to movement, sense experience, contemplation, and individual initiative. One has serious reservations about what sort of theology must be produced by the western "law of worship" construed as a "learning experience." One doubts that it would be construed as

4

orthodoxy in the traditional meaning of that term. Further reflection on this must be delayed for now, except to point out the obvious, namely, that meaning becomes delusion as it loses its connection to reality and falls under the sway of ideology, cant, and fads. Without recourse to reality, it is not possible to help the schizophrenic detect that his being Napoleon is an illusion, or to convince the Christian who has placed herself at the center of the cosmos that the Sabbath, while made for her, is not her plaything but her summons home to God.

Third, the author teaches in an interconfessional, university-based school of divinity. This means that he talks a great deal, perhaps more than one should, due to the vast differences in academic and religious background among his students. There is not much of a common language he and his colleagues can use to which all have access, so one must stretch vocabulary, explain everything, presume nothing. Baptism means one set of things to a Roman Catholic student, another to a Southern Baptist, a third to a Unitarian, and who knows what to a follower of the Reverend Moon. In this talky welter, one tosses words like broken bread on the waters. One cannot stop in the mere hope that students will make out of these fragments what they will. One must try to create a new language which will be accessible to diverse students and draw their various attitudes and interests into a new focus which will be worthwhile for the Gospel's sake. This sensed purpose causes us to deal more and more with basics which not too long ago were taken for granted. We ask ourselves what good there is in examining closely a crucial biblical text for one who has not only never read the book in which the text occurs but has never even read the Bible as a whole. Thus the move back to basics is not reactionary. It is only a necessary corrective to educational lacunae, similar to the faculty of an English

5

department making sure that its students are competent in the language before it asks them to understand Faulkner or write sonnets. The author is, in this sense, preoccupied with basics in the main line of Christian tradition East and West. In academe he wants to form students who will serve real congregations rather than be unleashed upon them. He would like to do the same during the course of this book.

Fourth, the author takes Christian asceticism seriously. Far from being something esoteric to Christianity, asceticism is native to the Gospel and is required of all. Specifically monastic asceticism was generated, it seems, in that same process by which living the Gospel began to take on ecclesial form in the earliest Jewish-Christian churches. So ascetical were these churches in the cultural milieux of their time that the early historian of Christianity, Eusebius, mistook the Jew Philo's description of Jewish ascetics for a description of Christian churches living the Gospel. Monasticism was not the creation of medieval bishops but of early Christian lay people. It flowed directly into Christian life out of Jewish prophetic asceticism which received new focus through the lens of Jesus' own teaching. One must therefore take the continuing fact of organized asceticism in Christian life as a given which provides access to whole dimensions of Christian perception and being. The existence, furthermore, of specifically monastic asceticism is a theological datum which lies close to the very nerve center of Christian origins and growth. One cannot study Christianity without taking monasticism into account. One cannot live as a Christian without practicing the Gospel asceticism which monasticism is meant to exemplify and support. A Christian need not be a monk or nun, but every monk and nun is a crucial sort of Christian, and there have been too many of these people over the centuries for their witness not to have considerable theological importance. Christianity's sustained ascetical stance, which is no less definite than a similar stance maintained in Buddhism and in Chinese Confucianism and classic Taoism, tells one something about the way any thoughtful person should address self and world, namely, with caution.

In light of all this, the author is a living paradox. The creature of a deeply sacramental tradition who works professionally in the symbolic liturgical expression of that tradition, he tries to affirm and commend the embrace of the world which that tradition and its liturgical expression would convey to others of Christian faith met for worship. Simultaneously, however, his own monastic engagement whispers in his ear that such an embrace must be undertaken not with reluctance but with a certain wariness. He is one in whom the tension between love of God's world and adamant critique of what we have made of it has taken on living form, reinforced by professional commitment to both sides of the tension. While he lives happily in the earthly city, he realizes that it does not abide and that his true enfranchisement is in another city which does abide but whose presence is not yet wholly consummated in space and time. Thus he finds himself committed to the human predicament. If the reader finds this book rather odd, this may be one reason why.

But there is one specific aspect of the way the author goes about things which the reader may find strange indeed, that is, the way he regards and assigns value to liturgical tradition. For him liturgical tradition is not merely one theological source among others such as various biblical theologies, patristic opinions, school emphases, or systems authored by this or that theological virtuoso. Rather he regards liturgical tradition, in whatever Christian idiom, as the dynamic condition within which theological reflection is done, within which the Word of God is appropriately understood. This is because it is in the Church, of which the liturgy is the sustained expression and the life, that the various sources of theology function precisely as sources.

This means that the liturgy of a church is nothing other than that church's faith in motion on certain definite and crucial levels. This faith surely has other modes and levels, but these are to be evaluated finally in terms of the church at worship before the living God, rather than vice versa. It cannot be forgotten that the church at worship is not only present to God; far more significantly, the living God is present to the church. This latter presence is not a theological theory; it is a real presence which is there to affect, grace, and change the world. It is an active real presence of God accomplishing his purpose as he will by the gift of himself in his Son through the Holy Spirit. God is not present to the worshiping church by faith but in reality; it is the church which is present by faith to God, and this faith reaches its most intense degree of relationship to its divine objective in a worshipful manner. No other stance is so appropriate when creature confronts Creator, when the redeemed regard their Redeemer.

Thus a church's worship does not merely reflect or express its repertoire of faith. It transacts the church's faith in God under the condition of God's real presence in both church and world. The liturgy does this to a degree of regular comprehensiveness which no other mode or level of faith-activity can equal. Therefore the liturgy is not merely one ecclesiastical "work" or one theological datum among others. It is simply the church living its "bread and butter" life of faith under grace, a life in which God in Christ is encountered regularly and dependably as in no other way for the life of the world.

Perhaps by now the reader can begin to grasp something of where I stand, if not completely how I stand it. The problem presented to me is how to express all this while maintaining a credible objectivity according to modern standards of academic scholarship.

These standards are relatively recent. To a large extent, they derive not from those in vogue until well into the Renaissance, standards which included not only truth but beauty and social congruence, but more from a concern which culminated in the elaboration of method in the natural sciences. This method requires dispassionate accuracy of observation, together with prediction of results verified by laboratory testing. Discrete truths are attained successfully using this method and they work with a bang in boardrooms and on battlefields. They can be photographed, popularized, and purveyed by the mass media. They can also be applied technologically and commercially to satisfy mass demand for products and services, thus creating the consumer base upon which western states rest and for which other modern states yearn.

Significantly, however, natural scientific method focuses less on truth itself than on truths which are probative. Scientific truth is less metaphysical and strategic than it is pragmatic and tactical, its vocabulary increasingly the statistic—a "word" whose existence is as undoubted as its place and relevance in the whole grammar of discourse is debated. Scientific truth is represented in a mushrooming lexicon which is as vast as its grammar is minimal. We seem to be sinking into a sea of "facts" which possess all the stunning power and incoherence of a novel by James Joyce or a play by Samuel Beckett. This makes it all the more difficult for those social agents of congruence—educational, political, religious—to accomplish their tasks and to maintain their credibility as they do so. Truth is balkanized, a condition which in turn suggests to some that truth itself is relative. This, when combined with modern science's avoidance of nonprobative issues such as beauty and social congruence, yields a peculiar and unstable culture which ordains its high priests on condition of their being so objective in their lack of passion as to be faceless. It is a culture in which everything works, but no one is willing to say why it ought to work; a culture which confuses truth with facts, builds machines to hold them, and then invests the machines with that numinousness which other cultures reserve for sages; a culture in which being wise means being smart about things which do not matter.

The intellectual ecology all this seems to cause is curious. It requires that a mind which lives in this ecology work at a distance from whatever the mind addresses. This is necessary in order that involvement with the object under study be avoided, lest accuracy in observation be compromised and prediction and verification collapse. Therefore anthropologists must study societies other than their own. What results is an outsider's impression of what goes on inside an alien human group. Tourists on a bus in Santa Fe have access through their books and guides to more facts about the rain dance they are watching through their windows than do the Indians themselves. But the tourists can never really know the dance as the dancers know it, and knowledge alone does not make tourists Indians. Yet our intellectual ecology pushes us to accept more readily the tourists' than the Indians' sort of knowing. Learned papers on the rain dance astonish no one more than Indians.

This is why what is done in divinity schools and seminaries is academically rather suspect, while what is done in departments of religious studies in state universities is not. Inmates of the former are Indians immersed in special pleading for facts they themselves create, predict, and verify. Their evidence on Christianity is not as dependable as that of a Tibetan Buddhist who visited one of them last year. The fact that he believes in reincarnation and prayer wheels somehow enhances his objective accuracy regarding Christian phenomena across the board.

It is patently ridiculous, and I do it myself all the time regarding my own tradition, so pervasive is the intellectual ecology in which I live and move and have my own academic being. It is why a respectable academician looks askance at Christian institutions in which tub-thumping fundamentalism is barely masked in caps and gowns. It is also why many unreligious moderns look at me and my colleagues in the same way. Perhaps all of us are not wholly in error. But it is clear that the modern demand for total, factual, and impersonal objectivity presents serious difficulties for one whose object of study is the faith in which one puts one's trust and to which one has dedicated one's life.

Which is to say that my colleagues and I have a problem when it comes to talking respectably about Church and World. I see three possible ways of handling this problem which may bear consideration.

First, one could get out of academe. I could retire to a hermitage in southern Indiana to contemplate and pray. I do feel at times, as did Thomas Aquinas toward the end of his life (when he was my age he had already been dead six years), that academical stuff is straw compared to what one glimpses, however darkly, in contemplation. Thomas himself took this course, dying not at his desk in Paris but in an obscure little Cistercian monastery in southern Italy, where he was lecturing to its few burly inmates on the Song of Songs. Church history is full of such people. Some of them became advocates of a holy Know-Nothingism. Some of them died from sheer relief. Some of them discovered in their solitude the blinding Truth which had eluded them in worldly careers.

One such was Evagrius of Pontus, who fled the business and fame of being archdeacon of Constantinople, where he had earned the sobriquet Destroyer of Heretical Twaddle, to become a monk in the deserts of Egypt. Here he distilled the first true synthesis of ascetical theory, a synthesis which has influenced either directly or indirectly all deep Christian spiritual writing East and West ever since. It entered southern France and Italy through his disciples Cassian and Palladius, where it seems to have been picked up by Benedict and made the center of his *Rule for Monasteries*. And without these monasteries, learning in the West might not have survived to produce the medieval universities and their Aquinases, their Luthers, their Calvins, their Cranmers, and eventually their Galileos and their Newtons. In short, the modern world. In view of all this, perhaps one should not dismiss too readily the advantages which may occasionally accrue from Christians getting out of academe. Christian asceticism, like the prospect of hanging, concentrates the mind and clears the head.

A second possibility is that a Christian might stay in academe and dissimulate belief. Such people are no doubt more numerous than those who get out of academe for ascetical purpose. They remain in academe and are worn down by it. Being worn down is often imperceptible in its slowness; it usually involves a transmutation of faith into one or more surrogates such as scholarship for its own sake, ideological distractions, or some form of involvement in activist causes of a political nature. The transmutation of faith into some surrogate is often accompanied, furthermore, by symptoms typical of transitions from one mode of life to another—symptoms of release, exhilaration, and freedom, a sense of new power, and feelings of having been "reborn." The transmutation is thus easily perceived as a conversion. And so it is, for conversion is a two-way street; whichever direction one takes produces largely the same feelings in the moving subject. One often encounters students who came to a seminary seeking less ordination than faith, only to discover counseling or social action as faith surrogates. One even encounters colleagues who at some point rise, as it seems, above faith only to vanish into therapy, eastern religions, another marriage, or some new ideology. Such folks, worn down by the unmanageable welter of modern academe, and dissimulating faith all the while in order to appear respectable, finally succumb to the lure of works which occupy but do not save. As Walker Percy says, they began by blowing their minds and end by blow-drying their hair. They leave us with neither insight nor faith, but with trivia of a certain passing interest.

A third possibility is that a Christian stay in academe and insist that his or her evidence be taken seriously. This is undoubtedly more difficult to do than the second possibility. It may even be more demanding in some ways than the first. It requires a high degree of ascetical study, disciplined methodology, a cold-eyed avoidance of sentimentality, prudent formulation of conclusions, steady regard of one's students and colleagues, and often courageous witness. Such work cannot stop with being highly professional. It must have vocation at its center; one must be called to it if one is to bear its stress. It is a grace one prays to receive and to sustain. What the ascetic contemplates, the Christian academic communicates. And the last may be even greater than the first since, as Aquinas points out, it is on the whole better to illuminate than to glow. Communicate, illuminate, witness. All these are active verbs which inevitably take a lot out of a person, as can be seen when one remembers that the old Christian word for witness is *martyr*, and that the greatest witness of all remains Jesus the Christ.

To what does a believing Christian witness in academe? Not to a Jesus of piety, I think, nor even to the Christ who can be known only by faith. These two all Christians share only with each other as colleagues in piety and faith. We do not write professional treatises on these for academic consumption for the same reason that lovers do not write white papers for each other on their love. We and they commune truly and deeply about these matters, but not in the same way professional academics do. Many things we say to each other in faith neither can nor should be said professionally in public. This is not to be secretive. It is merely to acknowledge that not everything which is felt can be said, and that not everything which can be said ought to be said in every forum, as Paul found out on the Areopagus.

To what, then, *does* a believing Christian witness in academe? To those modes of God's presence which are available to professional discourse and public bespeaking, namely, to Church and World. In these, and in all that each includes, the reality of God and his Christ becomes a public issue in a society's life and therefore falls within the realm of public discourse. Church and World are not mere adjuncts stuck arbitrarily onto God in Christ, nor are they mere signposts marking where God in Christ has passed but abides no longer. Rather, World is the fundamental mode in which the Creator manifests himself, infesting it with himself all the while. That infestation God brought to social focus slowly but elegantly first in humankind; then in a peculiar people, Israel; and finally within Israel to personal focus in his incarnate Son. It is this personal focus which became on the first

Pentecost perduringly social in a wholly new way. No longer humankind in general nor an ethnic group in particular, this new society emerged from the astonished confusion of a closed room as a new mode of God's focused presence in the World. It was the personal and "enfleshed" presence of the crucified and risen One given corporate form. As such, Paul saw this gathering, this *ecclesia*, so closely identified with him whom we all crucified that he felt compelled to call it his Body. By grace, faith, and sacrament, the Church is the fullness of him who is the fullness of the Godhead bodily. If the incarnation of the Logos was God enhumaned, the Church is God in Christ enworlded. It is with such modalities that human discourse can and must deal. Despite the objections of the hopelessly pious no less than of the hopelessly agnostic, the Unnameable in taking on such modalities becomes nameable, and human discourse is about naming.

This may serve as a pregnant if only initial clarification of how I regard what is possible for a believing Christian who does the academic thing. My nonbelieving colleagues and publics have no access, short of the grace of conversion, to the God and Christ of faith, while I do. But they and I together do have access to World and Church as concrete phenomena. I am obliged to be studious, methodical, unsentimental, prudent, and learned about both. And if I fulfill this obligation adequately, I see no reason why my evidence about both should not elicit similar address of Church and World from my unbelieving colleagues and publics. They may differ with my view of the World. They may remain dubious about the society I call the Church. But neither Church nor World are objects to which only the grace of faith gives access. Like Everest, they are there and exert causality in human affairs. Each demands our attention and can be spoken of according to standards of discourse no different from those we use concerning politics or economics, cabbages or kings. Unbelievers have no more special right to speak on politics than I have on Church. Both these things can be known if not fathomed. If known, they can be discoursed about with high discipline and definite results.

Unbelievers will have to construe their own problems with this according to their wits. The problems of believing Christians in academe are what concern me here. When it comes to discoursing about World and Church, we seem to have at least three problems.

The first problem is that of being objective. Being objective about what one lives in as deeply as World and Church is not easy. Objectivity is not a gift. It is a quality of mind which must be secured and then sustained only with constant effort. We in academe seldom notice its presence, only its absence, and its absence jars. Paradoxically, it is the very presence of objectivity concerning World and Church which often creates tension between those in academe and their coreligionists in parish and ecclesiastical bureaucracies. The objectivity with which we in academe must pursue our work simply to remain respectable is often an intimidation or a puzzle to them. They construe it as evidence that we have let them down somehow by not confirming, or by qualifying awkwardly, firmly held if not always adequately examined religious assumptions of their own. To do the academic thing in religion either presumes that one is in some tension with one's own official church, or that it will soon put one into this tension for worse or better. The first action the archbishop of Paris took in response to the death of Thomas Aquinas was to condemn his books. It has usually been so between chancery and university and I see no end to it. The two have come to work in different ways. No doubt each has much to learn from the other, but the learning has always been as hard as it has been sporadic.

This may itself be due to a second problem we have in discoursing about World and Church. It is that of theology as an academic endeavor, that is, theology as a task carried out in academe according to academic procedures and for academic, rather than pastoral or bureaucratic, ends. Many of us cannot conceive of theology otherwise, nor does it occur to us that theology ever was or can be done in any other way. This is not true. The academic structure we take for granted today as the locale for doing theology did not exist during the whole first half of Christianity's existence. Where analogues of modern academe can be found during that period, as in the Athens Academy which had its last surge of prestige under Julian the Apostate (331–363), they were populated less by believing Christians than by pagan advocates of the "old learning" and by gnostic dialecticians. This is not to say, however, that early Christian theologians were unlettered, even less that they were unintellectual. But they chose for the greatest part to do their work in settings other than the academies of their time. These settings were centers of Christian learning such as the catechetical schools of Alexandria, Antioch, and Milan, where the ends were more pastoral than academic. The greatest theologians of the era did their work in even more immediately pastoral settings—in the churches themselves, in pulpits on Sundays, amid catechumens preparing for baptism throughout the year, and in endless deliberative sessions adjudicating civil cases at law according to Christian principles. These legal involvements increased as civil authority slowly broke down in many parts of the late Roman empire, often leaving the local Christian bishop as the only figure with sufficient education and social prestige to uphold order. Augustine of Hippo complains repeatedly about the amount of time he had to spend in such activities.

It is worth remembering that the first syntheses of Christian theology were accomplished by people such as these. The ambience of their work was immediately pastoral, the purpose of their work was pastoral, they themselves were almost invariably pastors (i.e., bishops) and as often as not practicing ascetics who had to be forced into pastoral ministry against their wishes. Only three "world class" theologians during the first five or six centuries were not episcopal pastors: Tertullian, Origen, and Jerome. The inference that can be drawn from this is that theology was then regarded as a necessarily and intimately pastoral task, something regularly done by servants of the community, done live and in its solemn if often rowdy presence. The theology we today call patristic was thus a profoundly pastoral theology in its ambience, purpose, and execution.

This pastoral quality faded rapidly in the West as theology became focused in medieval universities under the scholastics, who were academics and almost never pastors. Theology began to withdraw from pulpits and the liturgy into the classroom and study. Thus a bifurcation in teaching functions set in and competing ways of going about reflection upon matters of faith and practice began to develop. The results of this are all around us today: a pastorate which, although not cut off altogether from the love of learning, has little time for learning's demanding practice and an academic structure with little real access to pastoral contexts in which the faith which theology is said to reflect upon is normally lived. Pastoral and theological disciplines are thus placed in a situation where it is almost impossible for them to interact upon each other except sporadically and, as it were, anecdotally. When the theological academy allows the pastoral field into its structure, its presence there is usually encased by conditions which assure that it will be unlikely to affect the conventional theological disciplines. The pastoral field in turn brings these restrictions upon itself by going about its business of flushing out problems and then attempting to deal with them by clinical and educational techniques which often betray little if any understanding of, or correlation with, theological discipline. Pastoral and theological enterprises thus lie tensely side by side or slide past each other, with few sparks leaping between them. Theology remains impervious to pastoral impregnation while the pastoral arts sink further into the strategic infecundity of clinicalism, educationalism, and personal idiosyncrasy.

The indictment here is not only of much which passes as "pastoral theology," but also of modern academic theology's pastoral astigmatism. Perhaps we who practice in academe do so in such a way that we suggest inadvertently to students that the real theological action is to be found only in academe. Thus our sharpest minds stay in academe. In this way we inbreed our craft and weaken pastoral ministry. It cannot be doubted that discovering a pastor or bishop with the theological acumen of a junior colleague, not to say of an Augustine or a Basil, is a rare event.[2] Both we in academe and they in parishes are to blame for this. One suspects that the nature of the modern academic theological enterprise may be central to our mutual difficulty.

A third and final problem affecting our ability to discourse professionally about Church and World may illustrate this difficulty. It is that of the priorities we assign to data in academic theology. In most schools of theology, the curriculum assigns highest priority to the studies of Bible and systematic theology about equally, perhaps with an edge given to biblical exegesis. History gets shorter shrift; cultural concerns such as anthropology and the arts, when they are taught at all, are most often electives; and the various pastoral crafts are taught in considerable array but usually remain at a distance from biblical and theological disciplines and tend to follow recent methodologies worked out in clinic and classroom. Due to its locale in the curriculum and to diverse methodologies, the pastoral area is ill-equipped to provide a unifying basis for all other studies even in those schools of theology which are especially devoted to training future pastoral ministers. It appears that the only areas which can do this are the biblical and theological disciplines. Thus the data they produce are regarded as premier in both research and pedagogy, not only in graduate schools of theology but in ministerial training programs as well.

Whether this arrangement is inevitable and permanent may be debated. But one thing it does is to render students initially adept as literary or intellectual critics of a special kind in biblical texts and the opinions of some theological authors. The pedagogical process is clear, disciplined, and demanding, but its results seem to be tactical rather than strategic. Techniques are transmitted but often fade or fall into disuse after graduation, and no story gets told. The biblical story of the World, the *mythos* which generates the Jewish and Christian worldview, seems to be presented not as a way of life but as a series of discrete if interesting problems. The history of the Church, the story which generates Christian identity and focuses Christian practice as a continuity of behavior, seems not to get told. Students are thrown back upon making up their own story or *mythos*, something which is governed less by academic biblical and theological analysis than by a continually shifting set of *ad hoc* influences, causes, ideologies, and temporary positions taken upon "issues." This results in a functional worldview constructed at some distance from both Church and academe, and made up of bits and pieces of civil religion, liberal or conservative establishmentarianism, good will, trendiness, subjectivist enthusiasms, and largely middle-class assumptions. The whole is kept in motion by a compulsive works-righteousness which would hardly be countenanced by any major Christian theologian past or present.

Perhaps we in academe have so specialized what we do that our corporate enterprise has become unable to narrate a story, to articulate a worldview, to profess a sense of World and Church in ways which make each accessible, not to say compelling, to our disciples. For all their apparent involvement in it, I sense that our students harbor a profound distrust of World. They tend to avoid entanglement in the compromises real politics always entail by becoming instead one-issue activists who will brook no compromise at all—a stance which seems to assault the political process rather than engage in it for a real, attainable, and thoroughly worldly common good. They also seem to harbor a profound distrust of Church as a let and hindrance upon their own creativity. They often come to ministry through a process of internal self-discovery which remains sovereignly "pure" of ecclesiastical entanglements. One student put it succinctly: "I think I have finally decided what my ministry will be. Can you suggest a church that will let me do it?" It cannot be ruled out that our students may perceive more accurately what we in academe are up to than we ourselves.

All this must bear heavily and often upon the mind of one who attempts to teach Christian worship in such a context. For Christian worship in its integrity is nothing if not both worldly and ecclesial. Furthermore, Christian worship seems to be, for reasons mentioned in the first part of this chapter, somehow primary and fundamental, rather than secondary and peripheral, to the whole theological enterprise. If this be true, then it would seem that addressing Christian worship possesses, at least in theory, greater prospects for unifying the academic theological curriculum than even biblical and theological disciplines, especially in schools which have ministerial training as their primary aim.

But this book is not about curriculum revision. It is about the possibility that liturgical worship, an endeavor both worldly and ecclesial, is itself fundamental to and constitutive of the faithful community and also of the ways in which that community reflects upon itself theologically. It seems best to begin pursuing this possibility by first looking at the World.

Chapter Two

The World

It is not possible to talk about Church without talking about World since Church exists in the World. World frames Church, and cosmology is the foundation on which ecclesiology rests.

This presents a pious and believing Christian in academe with some problems, not least among which is that classic Jewish and Christian theologies have not talked much about World in the way we do today. Modern natural science has given us a worldtalk which assumes that World is an impersonal object governed by inexorable forces about which we can do little if anything. Carl Sagan says of the physical universe that it is all there ever was, is now, and ever will be. Ostensibly for our benefit he then turned this vertiginous assertion into a sort of *son-et-lumière* electronic show which entertained, condescended to, and shrank its viewers to subatomic scale. In passing, it also cut them off from thousands of years of hard religious thought which, paradoxically, laid the groundwork for modern science by embracing World as rather more than a merely physical universe.

Religious systems have tended to approach World less as an impersonal object than as the subject of what personality, divine and human, would make of it. For them, World is not merely a given but artifact. Judaeo-Christianity has spoken of World not just as physical universe but as a creation by some One and as the playground of Wisdom. And classic Christianity, an urban endeavor from its earliest days, has seen the two main foci upon that playground in urban terms as *civitas terrena* or *hominum* and as *civitas Dei*. In this view, the universe of things and forces, so far from being Sagan's impersonal object, is an artifact of divine and human intelligence; something shot through with intelligibility in each and all its parts, an intelligibility which often goes beyond what can be known in laboratory and study or by human minds alone. The workshop in which all this intelligibility is discovered and shaped into accessible form lies at the center of every human community and is the central concern of every human group, the locale of human endeavor par excellence. This endeavor is the fundamental human craft, and it is carried on by a complex series of interlocking transactions with reality which, because of their communal and social scope, are "political" in nature. Splendid minds from Moses to Aristotle to Einstein, from Lao Tsu to the Gautama to Michelangelo and even Sagan do not wander in from jungles or drop from the skies. They are products of their cultures' transactions with reality, and so were their anonymous colleagues who aeons before them spun the first wheel, first lit a fire, first planted a seed, domesticated the dog, rode a horse, spoke the first word, scratched out the first letter, added the first sum, laid out the first city, and offered the first sacrifice.

All these are social effects. They are at the same time social causes, for when one transacts with reality, a thing causes to the extent that it is the effect of what precedes it. Think of $E = mc^2$. Think of *sacramenta significando efficiunt gratiam* (sacraments by signifying effect grace). Neither of these formulations fell from the sky wrapped in plastic. They emerged from countless transactions with reality carried on over millenia in the central workshops of the human *civitas*, and each has transformed that *civitas* for worse or better. For this reason if for no other, when one enters these workshops one walks on holy ground—which is why the race has always regarded its cities as dynamic and holy icons of the World.[3]

Until recently.

When Rousseau taught in the eighteenth century that the *civitas* of human society corrupts, he gave philosophical voice to a religious suspicion which had taken root in late medieval Christianity out of frustration with its hypertrophied and already crumbling *civitas*. By the sixteenth century, sensitive Christians had already begun to trek out of their city in search of No Place, *outopos*, Utopia. Many of them found it in the human individual standing pure, noble, and brave outside town, in deep and exclusive dialogue with the God of Moses alone atop Sinai, with the God of Jesus alone on Calvary—by the grace of faith alone, forswearing civil discourse. This was called "modern devotion" at the time, and the splendor of its piety cannot be gainsaid. But it was perhaps where Rousseau's noble savage was begotten. His existence was confirmed in the discoveries of South Seas explorers, which stunned and fascinated Europe during the first half of the eighteenth century as moon landings have fascinated us in the twentieth. Tahiti (which was cityless) was Utopia, wrote one explorer, "the one spot upon the earth's surface without either vices, prejudices, wants or dissension." Defoe and Swift novelized on the subject, French encyclopedists philosophized on it, and Americans such as Jefferson embedded the vision in their new nation's lore of distrust for things urban and of favor for all things and persons rural. Until well into this century, an American had difficulty in being elected president without some demonstrable link to noble savagery represented in frontier background, birth in a log cabin, or origin in the *rures*. In Europe, Rousseau's noble savage became what Camus would call "the hero of our times," fashioned into a political superman by Hegel, Nietzsche, and Marx; into a cultural hero by Oscar Wilde; into a type of perfect Christian, unrepressed, shameless, and guilt-free by D.H. Lawrence; into the bearer of power once attributed to God by Feuerbach, Sartre, and modern Existentialists.

The upshot of all this is not merely that such an exalted creature has in our own day been transmuted into the terrorist or "freedom fighter" on the one hand, or been trivialized by entertainment media into the "Dukes of Hazzard" on the other. The more strategic effect of all this is that the city as World icon is being destroyed, not by being secularized (it was always secular at base with some sacral potencies shooting through it from every angle) but by being radically profaned. The city has become the playground not of Wisdom but the battleground of savages, as in Belfast and Beirut. The city's sacral potentialities have been removed and invested in the sovereign individual. Its central workshop, where radical transactions with reality used to summon a citizenry to meet in peace, was given notice that its lease was up. The center gave way to parking lots and bus stops; discourse fractured, politics increasingly issued from the mouths of ideological gurus, and the sovereign individual was relegated to suburban sprawls focused on centers of consumption called shopping malls. Here anxiety and frustration mounted as identity waned. The noble savage, afrolic upon the breast of Nature, began to grasp dimly that he had come to be regarded by government as a statistic, by business as a tangle of glands and urges, by society as a case for study, and by ideological gangs as a hostage to their own totalitarian ends.

In a denouement of major proportions it seems that the noble savage in our day has been shorn of his nobility and some of his savagery. The monstrous Adolf Eichmann, on lengthy examination at his trial for genocide in 1958, was found to be in fact little more than a petty bureaucrat distinguished only by an absence of thoughtfulness which seemed to deaden whole areas of his perception of reality.[4] He was possessed by a certain impersonal fatalism that rendered his evil banal: a whole people had to be obliterated not because of some fulminating ideology, but merely because the last official order in triplicate from the front office required it. Eichmann's interest was piqued only by how such an order might be carried out in the most cost-effective manner. Savagery bought itself a leisure suit and moved in next door.

The most fundamental reason for this development seems to be neither theological nor religious at base, but psychosocial. It results in a loss of faith, but the scope of this loss is not restricted to the religious sphere alone. As Hannah Arendt has noted, even if we admit that the modern age began with a sudden, inexplicable eclipse of transcendence, " . . . it would by no means follow that this loss threw men back upon the world. The historical evidence, on the contrary, shows that modern men were not thrown back upon this world but upon themselves. One of the most persistent trends in modern philosophy has been an exclusive concern with self, as distinguished from the soul or person or man in general, an attempt to reduce all experiences, with the world as well as other human beings, to experiences between man and himself. The greatness of Max Weber's discovery about the origins of capitalism lay precisely in his demonstration that an enormous, strictly mundane activity is possible without any care for or enjoyment of the world whatever, an activity whose deepest motivation, on the contrary, is worry and care about the self. World-alienation, and not self-alienation as Marx thought, has been the hallmark of the modern age."[5]

If this is true, it means that modern "secularism" is not worldliness but unworldliness. Its icon is not a city, whether of man or God, but the lone runner jogging through suburbia in order, we are told, to feel good about himself. These people we lionize in marathons organized and run at public expense. It also implies that the person is probably adrift upon a sea of options which have meaning only to the extent that they are chosen by the sovereign individual. "Real people" are regarded as existing prior to social discourse with others. This gives rise to the impression that whatever evils there may be are rooted in impersonality; that closeness between persons is requisite; that such closeness must be immediate and primary, and that this is the only way one grows—by sharing the unspoken with the unspoken-to (the most important things, we say, cannot be put into words). Anything that intrudes into this exclusive and fairly aphasic bond between sovereign individuals imperils the bond and is therefore oppressive—social things especially, such as customs, manners, law, role, reverence, even grammar. This produces people who are awash in an oceanic ideology of shifting intimacy which is replete with uncontrolled, unanchored, and undirected sacralities. It is unworldly to the point of being creepy, for what it amounts to is the effacement of the *res publica* by the preference to believe that social meanings are generated only by the feelings of individual human beings. If one feels oppressed, one is oppressed, and the oppression is by definition the effect of social constraint.

In such situations, few transactions with reality are socially possible and communicable except through channels which have been ideologically reformed and greatly constricted. One such channel is Business reformed as *res publica*: the business of America, said Calvin Coolidge, is Business. The reform has been from business as people effecting transfers of wealth for goods and services, to Business as a set of abstract economic "forces" severely regulated by ideologies given political, and then governmental, shape in the form of this or that policy. The ideological basis of these policies becomes clear when it is realized that, whether or not they work for the common good according to empirical tests, they must nonetheless continue to be regarded as valid in their own right, as dogmatic propositions to which all owe assent. This dogmatic level constrains the reform of Business already mentioned and removes it as a proximate threat to the sovereignty of the individual, who now may not lose income due to shifts in demand for goods and services or to inefficiency in meeting the demand, even if the general public must subsidize the loss. Wealth and its increase is guaranteed, while responsibility for its production is located elsewhere than in the competence, efficiency, and responsibility of the individual. The sovereign individual is freed as society is bent to his service. One asks not what one can do for the common good, but what the common good, the oppressor par excellence, can do for one.

Another such channel is Science. Reformed by modern positivism, Science is constrained from dealing with such septic concerns as aesthetic and social congruence. It is regarded as being in the very nature of scientific knowing that there can be no indwelling participation of the knower in the achievement and account of that knowledge. It is a knowledge which is supposed to be achieved by an intellect liberated from personal direction and human bias; an intellect, in short, which observes the world as if the intellect were not present in it; an intellect which should be able to reduce its account of knowledge drawn from disinterested observation to binary numbers processed in electronic devices. Unlike the human city, modern Science is not only unhumane but unworldly as well. The *civitas* may watch science being done, pressing its nose to the glass as in Sagan's popular television series. But the *civitas* may never be allowed to participate, lest the purity of the scientific distillation be compromised by civil involvement. Meanwhile, the sovereign individual is encouraged to nurture the confident expectation that his or her life can be made only better through chemistry.

Since the common good has been redefined by a reformed and constrained Business, the workshop of the *civitas* must be remodeled by the modern State to secure, coercively when necessary, that redefined common good, with Science as the aloof and impersonal provider of weapons and techniques for the State to use in its coercive functions. High on the State's list of opponents in this endeavor are those older public agents such as the family, neighborhood, ethnic group, and Church. In the old *civitas*, these mediated between State and individual by way of local precinct, party politics, parish, and every local chapter of paralegal or even illegal *famiglia*. Under the new governance of affairs, the State must either neutralize or destroy these mediating agencies so that it can have direct and exclusive access to the individual, who comes to be regarded less in human, moral, and aesthetic terms than as an impersonal consuming unit of material goods and services. The old professions, which were once also mediating agencies between the larger community and the individual, are transmuted into mere trades which facilitate the delivery of material goods and services: professors and teachers deliver "educational services," doctors and nurses deliver "health-care services," clergy deliver "pastoral-care services," lawyers deliver "legal services," and all such persons are regarded as possessing "skills" which are marketable. Both the skills and their results have been redefined in mercantile terms which make them all liable to State constraint. Armed by Science, the modern State coerces the individual no longer with rack and rope but with chemical or electronic narcotics, statistics, tax policies, arcane dogmas, behavior modification techniques, and finally with the threat not of penitentiary but of institutional "therapy."

Radical transactions with reality in the *civitas* have given way to manipulation of the individual according to standards approved not by humane, because civil, discourse but by the vast and impersonal forces of Business, State, and Science. Those agencies which most obviously oppose these forces, moreover, often become no less inhumane or unworldly than those forces themselves. Special interest groups and one-issue political coalitions take nonnegotiable stands based on irreducible demands formulated out of social dogma. It is as though such coalitions regard their own standards as so impeccable as to be quite above the vulgarity of political intercourse, the very essence of which is compromise in favor of the common good. These groups wish to dictate what the common good is to be. And while such groups may often act and sound "political," they are in fact private eschatological totalitarianisms whose tactics are pious aggression. Rather than being effective challenges to Business, State, and Science, such coalitions seem actually to enhance the hold these three have upon the *civitas* by, like them, assaulting the political process rather than enhancing it.

At least part of the bill the *civitas* must pay for this is mounting social disaffection which takes the form of what Richard Sennett has called a culture of negation. Business, State, and Science are, like Mother Nature, perilous to touch, and when one or another of them fail no one is responsible. Inmates of such an impersonal order defend themselves in their impotence by declaring their masters and their manipulating systems illegitimate. Authority in such a case does not merely lapse; it is perceived increasingly as malign. The perception forces authority to take one of two courses: to become paternalistic in order to ameliorate its critics and tie them more closely to itself; or to become increasingly totalitarian in order to control its critics and stifle their criticism. In either case, fresh credibility is given to the central delusion of enlightenment, romantic, and revolutionary legacies deriving from Rousseau, namely, that disbelief in authority brings freedom, equality, and fraternity just as distance from the human *civitas* assures individual integrity and human authenticity.

This narrative, which has now returned to its starting point, is patently not exhaustive, nor is it very nuanced. But perhaps it will suffice to suggest some of the reasons why our view of the World as it is in itself, and apart from our feelings toward it, seems to be in difficulty. It is a view which has become myopic and foreshortened. When we venture beyond the borders of our own sovereign subjectivity, we do so with about as much confidence and gusto as would have been possible for Harriet Beecher Stowe on a tour of Sicily. So apparently intimidating is the world-beyond-ourselves that we feel it necessary not just to reduce it to human scale (something which all cultures attempt to do), but to trivialize it into some form of entertainment which we can share in vicariously and at a distance, or to break it down into a set of atomized "options" which we remain free to change according to whim. Although we are in it, we are not of it. It does not create us, nor we it. We create ourselves apart from it and in spite of it. It exists for us to do with as we please, when we please, if we please. Business, protected by a State armed by Science, reduces the World to consumer units, which we may then purchase and enjoy and throw away.

We have moved out of the *civitas* of World into a suburbia of sovereign subjectivity where the air is better for genteel savages whose individuality is absolute, sovereign, and weirdly noble. From here the view is frosty clear and the old *civitas* can be seen for the trap and delusion it always was, a vast stew of tarts, muggers, ethnics smelling of garlic or collard greens, religious primitives, and ward heelers—cosmic unfortunates for whom, tiresomely, we the enlightened are obliged to care until their ability to breed can be curtailed. Unless they can become aseptic and anonymous citizens of the new electronic city they have no business existing. They are evolutionary dead ends.

This brings us to a very hard question indeed. Who is really the evolutionary dead end after all? Modern science is a help at this point. Human evolution, it points out, began not in a neat suburbia, but in terrestrial swamps from which crawled not housewives in slacks and husbands in baseball caps but newts clothed in nothing but warts and slime.

The book of Genesis does not differ much from this. We began, it says, not in the antisepsis of a laboratory but as a mud pie shaped by the same Force which either called or pushed the first newt out of a swamp put there for that very purpose. Newts and we rejoice in the same source. The same swamp is our common home, and both of us came out of it wearing similar suits of clothes. The only significant difference between us, says Genesis, is that the newt did not name us, but we it. In doing so, we took our first step into cooperation with the purposeful meaning the Creator had injected into every nook and cranny of creation.

Made somehow in the Creator's image, we began to act in the Creator's image. When we named the newt, the *civitas* was conceived, a terrestrial entity giving form to the World born from the Creator's womb.

Genesis is the first of three books in the Jewish and Christian library of sacred books which bear in particular the burden of the World's story. The second book is its recapitulation and consummation, the Apocalypse. The third is the epistle to the Hebrews. Genesis is *alpha*, Apocalypse *omega*. But Hebrews is the hinge that joins the other two together. Genesis says that we began in a swamp teeming with life, but that something went vastly wrong one evening at dinner. Apocalypse says that the difficulty was finally resolved into something called the Banquet of the Lamb. Hebrews tell how the resolution was accomplished, not in an orchard set in pleasant countryside but in a butcher shop located in the city's center. The World's story from beginning to end pivots upon this resolution, a resolution the faint of heart, the fastidious, and the squeamish find hard to bear. Suburbia prefers its meat wrapped in plastic, all signs of violence removed so as to reduce the necessity of entering into the dark and murderous transaction with reality which one creature's giving up its life for another entails.

Hebrews insists that the transaction cannot be avoided. Hebrews also insists that the transaction lies at the heart of what we have made of the World, and therefore of ourselves, beginning at that first unpleasantness at dinner and stretching even into the final Banquet, which is even now begun. Hebrews summons us to this appalling transaction because we are a bloody bunch who have made the World a bloody place both for ourselves and for every other creature we have named. Every dish on our table contains something which has died violently at our hand. We are not constitutionally angels but omnivorous carnivores. We are not, however, constitutionally murderers; this we are by choice and delectation. We have an alarming propensity to slay not to stay alive, but for the sheer hell of it. This is the core of our problem: not whether or not to slay, but slaying rightly or wrongly.

To slay rightly is to transact the inexorable business of life. The fruit our first parents ate died in its own fruitness to live on in their lives. The wrongness of their act lay not in appropriating the life of the Tree for themselves, but in their doing so for ends other than the transaction allowed. They committed quiet, permissible, and necessary violence in the World, but they did it against the World's common good and in violation of its contractual foundation. They slew and ate a living worldly thing to be like God, something which fruit, even in the glory of its creaturehood, could not give. The slaying was thus wanton and unjust because it was out of proportion to its reason. The fruit could sustain our first parents' life in the World. It could not give them uncreated life beyond this World.

Our first parents perverted food and thus sinned against the Creator by sinning against creation. The communion of all in all was ruptured. Names lost their power to designate cleanly, relationships warped, and the means of life mutated into means of death. Our means of sustenance were poisoned. *Lebensbaum* became *Totesbaum*, and our transactions with reality degenerated into a drunken brawl across tables soaked in blood—our own and that of everything else. Our contracts became illegible under bloody fingerprints, our eyes bloodshot, our heads throbbing with a hangover nothing could dispel. We went to our own deaths kicking and screaming, or with mute resignation, because we had made death into little more than a capricious and useless rape of life. And we found ourselves sitting amid piles of cosmic wreckage trying to remember how things had come to such a pass.

To deal with this situation, we fled the inhospitable chaos of the wilderness into cities. Perhaps together we could there bring some order into the mess, at least temporarily. But whenever we seemed to succeed in this aim, however briefly, we found our yen for blessed order both increased and frustrated, for what we touched always receded beyond our grasp. The true city we were attempting to secure was always unattainable, retreating over the nearest horizon or floating just out of reach. But we could see enough of it to discern its external aspects, and we modeled what city we had to resemble it somewhat, even if our own city contained little more at its heart than a graveyard where our deepest aspirations lay entombed.

This situation was intensified when on occasion the Creator relented and began to camp out in our midst. Then we began to see what the center of our stillborn city might be like. It would be a teeming bazaar where our race might transact radical business with reality in the solemn presence of reality's Source. We tried various media of exchange: money, promises, good intentions. None worked to our ultimate satisfaction. It finally occurred to us that the transaction had to cut closer to the bone, involving the very root of our miserable condition. We had to learn how to slay rightly again, to commerce in vital deaths so that the communion of all in all might be restored. There could be no shortcuts. We had to look the lamb in the eye as we cut its lovely throat, and we had to keep that awful memory as we dined thankfully upon its flesh to live. Without this unspeakable memory, we found that we grew quickly cold once again—calculating, unworldly about World, forgetful that the carrots we pulled in our gardens and the wheat we cut in our fields died no less really than the lamb of liquid eye so that we might live. And we entertained the distant possibility that our own lives might have to be yielded up in the same spirit for the life of all; that, as someone finally said, we could discover life only in throwing it away.

The choreography of all this is what Hebrews describes. It is the World's existential dance, its cosmic Goldberg Variations, the solemn liturgy no longer of a lamb led to sacrifice but of a perfect Lamb who leads all of us to the World's altar and then concelebrates there his own sacrifice with all that is. Here alone can the mess of Genesis finally resolve into Apocalypse's Banquet of the Lamb. Here alone our own fragile *civitas* is transmuted into *civitas Dei*. Here alone the world as sin and the world as creaturely good news are restored to each other as one World. Here alone are we able to transact business with reality on the most radical level. Looking that Lamb in the eye, we discover ourselves as we always had been to One who abides beyond our limits in space and time. And in that Lamb's death, searing in its simplicity, we came home. Our city had found its heart. Its name was Sion, and in Sion's midst there was standing a Lamb as it were slain.

All this is completely worldly. It accounts for the World in worldly terms, permitting no unworldly *deus* or even *homo ex machina*. It regards our race as presiding not over World but within World as the firstborn of living creatures and responsible for them all to their Source.

It recognizes that humanity exercises its peculiar role in creation only corporately, socially, not by imposition from without but by necessity from within. "God created man in his own image, in the image of God he created him; male and female he created them." Created personhood is a community of persons and "man" is plural. It is as though when it comes to person, the deity knows of no option other than to create such a thing corporately, the deity itself being a community of Persons. It must be inferred, therefore, that the social taproot of the human *civitas* sinks itself not merely into man's corporate personhood of male and female, but even into the more intimate community of Persons in one nature which is the Godhead itself. God, no less than man, is a collective being, and the words for each are collective nouns. The divine community refracts itself in space and time as human community. We are God's finite extrapolation, as *civitas hominum* is the finite extrapolation of *civitas Dei*. When we walk in our city, therefore, we walk always on holy ground.

To realize this is to grasp something of the World. For this reason it seems that Judaeo-Christianity among all the world's religious traditions is congenitally the most worldly and the only one which is fundamentally urban. What this implies in practice can perhaps be sketched when it comes to describing the Church.

Chapter Three

The Church

*"You are the light of the world. A city set on a mountain
cannot be hid."*

Matthew 5:14

Judaeo-Christianity has never been overly concerned
with idioms of religious experience which are
exclusively rural. It has been hostile to fertility rites
performed in fields at springtime. It has rejected out of
hand religious preoccupations with time as a closed
cycle based on the inevitable recurrence of natural
seasons of growth and decay.

This reserve regarding rural idioms has suggested to
some, in particular those romantics who exalt the noble
savage afrolic upon the breast of Nature, that Judaeo-
Christianity is a religion which stands in opposition to
Nature and to World; a religion governed by a God-
idea expressed in oppressive commandments against
natural enjoyments at its beginning, by an alien Savior-
God who pops in and out of the World at its middle,
and directed by a mirthless series of hierarchs toward
its end, an end administered at last by Darwin and
given *coup de grâce* by Einstein and modern Science.

This perception is mistaken. Judaeo-Christianity is not
uncaring about whales and organic farming. It merely
regards them as not the Problem. Judaeo-Christianity
regards humanity and its City as the Problem at the
center of the World. It has addressed this Problem with

sustained intensity for some 4,000 years in a discourse which is all but erotically entwined with things, and with images of things, during the whole time. The discourse has been on the whole tougher and more disciplined than the average romantic has been able to detect. Jews and Christians have tended not to talk so much about the meaning of things in themselves, but rather to presume that their meaning is contained simply in their creaturely existence, to revere that existence, and then to bless their Creator for it. "Blessed be the Lord God, King of the universe, for the fruit of the vine. Blessed be he."

But Jews and Christians start talking very much indeed when it comes to imaging things, because the act of imaging is itself a human construction with which we endow things in our necessary use of them, and the act of imaging may be for worse or better. It seems to be at this point, where a created thing is raised by us to the level of human artifact, that Jews and Christians become concerned. When grape drippings become wine, when grain becomes bread, when color and surface become icon—that is, when the human *civitas* makes—then the discourse heats up. When things get put into relationships with other things and with us under our agency, they become capable of freeing us or of reducing us into bondage. At this point they take on meaning which is no longer only the Creator's but ours as well. And here is where the snake, our household pet, joins the transaction.

I am saying that a completely "natural" grasp of created things—from neutrons to suns, from cabbages to whales—is relative and illusory; that we make of things what we will; that it takes so high a discipline to keep from perverting them to our own doom that we cannot carry it on without significant help from beyond ourselves (which is about as circumlocutory a way of saying "grace" as one is apt to get). A human artifact is necessarily to some extent sacrament, that is, an artificially induced relationship of goods which human agency freights with significance vital or fatal. Judaeo-Christianity is in this perspective a religious tradition which is not only wordly and urbane but immersed in artistic discourse. This is one way of saying that the common tradition is thoroughly sacramental. It may not be altogether hostile to other forms of discourse. It just does not find them very interesting. What it does find interesting is how we keep our necessary but artificial agency in creation from doing us in.

This may be regarded as a fairly arrogant thing to say, so I should perhaps contrast sacramental discourse with another sort of artistic discourse, painting. Leonid Ouspensky has noted that according to the laws of optics the dimensions of objects decrease with distance and the lines of perspective cross each other at the horizon.[6] Every painter knows this and uses it to suggest depth, a third dimension in only two. But the icon painter inverts this. His point of departure in perspective is not found in the illusory depth of the image which attempts to reproduce visible space, but before the image, in the spectator himself. Referring to the seventh ecumenical council's emphasis on the perfect correspondence between icon and holy scripture, by which the icon is regarded as calling one to the life which God's Word reveals, Ouspensky points to an analogous inversion of things in the Gospel. There, everything is in the same inverse perspective: the first shall be last, the powerless rather than the powerful shall inherit the earth, and the humiliation of the cross is the supreme victory.

The lessons of the painter are learned from Nature. The lessons of the iconographer are learned in the City's center, to be upended by grace and expressed by inverting perspective. Painting and icon are both artifacts, but the latter is raised to the level of high

41

sacrament. It is a faith-made thing, the result of a supremely civil transaction with the real and done in the city center of the World changed in Christ. So too are bread and wine, oil and water. Every sacrament, being an act of faith, inverts the perspective natural to humanity's city, putting the cross of Christ not on the distant horizon of possible human options but deep into the mind and heart of the spectator who comes close to it in faith. It kills in order that life might flow. Nothing else, in a sacramental context, is of such high interest, nothing else an option.

This suggests that I should hold three positions.

First, I should hold that those who live close up to the icon of the Gospel by faith, and who are thus the focus of its inverted perspective, constitute the Church. The cross of Christ plunges into them by a conversion which they seal under God by baptism into the death of him who is by nature and vocation the World's Good News and Anointed One, the Messiah-Christos of God. His cross embeds itself in them by grace and a faith-filled life consummated each Sunday as they banquet in thanksgiving upon his body broken and his blood poured out for the life of the world. This seems to imply that the Church as a faith-society is sacramental in its very constitution, and that it functions as a many-faceted, dynamic, and corporate sacrament in its own right. That is, it functions as a vast mystery which itself inverts perspective, projecting World out of Gospel rather than Gospel out of World.

Second, I should hold that such a Church is the central workshop of the human City, a City which under grace has already begun to mutate by fits and starts into the City-of-God-in-the-making, the focal point of a World made new in Christ Jesus. It is a City whose populace is *simul justus et peccator*, filled with both saints and sinners, all of whom constitute the central workshop's clientele. This is because it is not fundamentally the Church which has been redeemed in Christ but the World itself. A redeemed World makes its own peculiar City, a City which then stands as artifact and icon of such a World. And such a City requires that its central workshop do certain things in certain ways. The World sets the City's agenda, an agenda which is then executed in the City's workshop, the Church. The scope of this agenda is such that the Church must first of all be and act in a manner which is catholic, that is, Citywide and Worldwide in its nature and ends. Catholicity is a quality endowed upon Church by City and World. It is not a quality which the Church generates for itself, in its own self-interest according to criteria which are the Church's own. If the Church is found to be concerned with reconciling its members, this is because the Church is servant of the reconciliation already accomplished constitutionally by Christ Jesus between his Father and this World, this human City. The Church and sectarianism are thus antithetical entities, and that the Church Catholic is one denomination among others, a sort of religious boutique in the suburbs, is an unthinkable proposition. When the Church fails at being catholic, it begins to fail at being one, holy, and apostolic as well. The Church as central workshop is crucial not merely to the well-being of redeemed World and City but to the very existence of both.

The brunt of all this is that, third, I should hold that the work and discourse of the City's central workshop, the Church, must be congruent with the work and discourse of City and World. This work and discourse is carried on by a vast interlocking series of transactions with reality, transactions consummated politically, socially, philosophically, and morally in continuity with what went before, so that what may occur in the future will happen for the good of the entire *res publica*. When an architect builds and a politician proposes, for example, they do so not merely in converse with themselves. They work to provide spatial and social order for people to act in. Their discourse is never asocial or value free, therefore, for all such orderings are acts of World-construction within a civil frame. To build otherwise assaults the World by violating the City's iconic function. To secure the World by compromising the City is to secure nothing but one's own alienation from the City, one's own isolation in the World. The transaction can never be with one's own creative impulse alone. It must be with nothing less than the real, both socially and universally perceived. The results of doing less are all around us in unlivable cities and in societies which endow their inmates with little more than pathological levels of anxiety and a sense of being somehow oppressed.

The Church cannot allow itself to do less instead of enough. To fulfill its obligation to the good of the entire redeemed *res publica*, the Church also must transact with the real—not with exclusivist urgings within its own sense of creativity, not with false cosmologies, not with dubious theologies. Its guide in the matter is primarily the Gospel perceived and received worshipfully as it stands before the living God in Christ; reverently, prayerfully, effacing itself by abnegation and candor. To perceive and receive the Gospel this way is to perceive and receive it socially in the midst of graced believers, the saints and sinners who together are the corporate locale of Christ's life-giving Spirit. The Church's transactions, like those of all the City's citizens, must be with nothing less than the real both socially and universally perceived, the social and cosmic dimensions of its work acting as effective controls upon its lapsing into self-aggrandizing solipsism. This last begins to occur precisely to the degree that the Church allows itself by pious fits to float free of World and City, becoming thereby unworldly, spiritualized, abstracted, idealized, sectarian, and gnostic.

When this happens, and to whatever degree it happens, the Church's discourse about its work moves similarly from a worldly to an unworldly vocabulary. The discourse becomes precious, aseptic, notional. Adjectives increase as verbs and nouns decrease. The workshop relocates to suburbia and becomes no longer a civic affair but a series of cottage industries producing novelties and fads for passing elites. The workshop's products cease to be plumbing systems which make the City work. They are rarefied into luxury items for the jaded, collectibles for the curious. As the Church withdraws to the City's outskirts, moreover, the center of town is left in the hands of thugs and the disenfranchised. Farmers sell off their land and move into the inner city, where they are unemployable; city dwellers flee into the now vacant *rures*, where they do not know how to farm. The City collapses. Then the World becomes unknowable and inaccessible, a great dead corpse upon which the loathsome feed.

In such a perspective, the Church is not an option in a redeemed World any more than is the City. All three are necessities. To discourse about any one of them is to discourse simultaneously about the other two on distinct but inseparable levels. This is why Christian discourse is radically symbolic. Symbols fold in much meaning from different levels rather than exclude it. Such discourse is necessarily paradoxical and universal without falling into contradiction or illogic. It has to say that, like Jesus, it comes to bring not peace but violence, that the incomprehensible has become knowable, that securing life requires throwing it away, that death lies behind rather than before a believer in Jesus the Christ. Poets, musicians, dancers, and artists know this sort of thing well because their craft cannot be practiced without such knowledge. That so many Christians have come to forget this is, it seems, one result of our having allowed the Church to withdraw into the suburban confines of our own minds, where it becomes our creation rather than we its creation.

Yet traditional Christian discourse has been far more rich, complex, and flat-footedly objective than any individual mind can comprehend. Its discourse is sacramental because it is symbolic, and it is this sort of discourse *necessarily*. I take this therefore to be utterly primary, basic, and fundamental for ecclesiology. This sacramental discourse transcends and subordinates the discourse of academic theological reflection on the Church, just as the law of worship transcends and subordinates the law of belief: *lex supplicandi legem statuat credendi*, a civil and worldly statement if ever there was one.

It would be foolish not to recognize that placing sacramental discourse prior to, above, and in a role which subordinates theology in the modern academic sense is a difficult if not incomprehensible move for many people. We generally think of the two sorts of discourse the other way around, theology coming first and sacramental discourse very much later as a possibly implied excursus off the former. Sacramental discourse in fact is often thought of as theological adiaphora best practiced by those with a taste for banners, ceremonial, and arts and crafts. It is regarded as an academically less than disciplined swamp in which Anglican high churchmen, Orthodox bishops, and many if not all Roman Catholics and others are hopelessly mired.

A good example of this attitude is the following description in the catalogue of a certain academic institution for summer course 106, "Creative Worship":

"How to creatively use liturgy, liturgical robes, banners and stoles in both worship and church school. Discover exciting 'tools' for spreading the Good News!"

Besides being marginally literate, the description cannot bear much scrutiny, because the notion of Church which lies behind it seems to be that of an ecclesiastical boutique. The relationship of embroidery to the driving of a diesel locomotive seems easier to demonstrate than the connection between stoles and proclaiming the Gospel. Something here seems to have been enthusiastically trivialized. Incongruities are joined, reality warped, meaning maimed. Artifact becomes plaything, *sacramentum* a rubber duck.

Human language about wordly matters such as reality, life and death, City and Church, always goes "sacramental" when it gets beneath mere surface appearances. Scientists start talking about charmed quarks; Christians start talking about tombs and wombs. While the City may often seem little more than a cluster of stores and alleys, it is more than this because people live and work there, and their corporate aspirations image the City as exalted, timeless, with streets of gold and walls of precious stones, a heavenly Jerusalem. While the Church may often seem little more than an institution like all others, it has from the beginning been deemed more than that because its members are graced people. St. Paul called it a Body, a mysterious entity to which only the intimate metaphor of marriage between man and woman, that primordial human society, gives access.

In the case of City and Church, the need to image in order to know gives rise to special sorts of discourse which are more necessary than optional. The discourse thickens meaning found in reality and then increments that meaning with style. People do this sort of thing when statements of mere fact fail due to the complexity

of what the statement needs to express. It is not poetry
to report the fact that I love someone. It is poetry to say
"How do I love thee? Let me count the ways . . . ."
Meaning is being thickened and is about to be
incremented with style. Again, it is not poetry to report
that one stopped for the evening. But it is poetry to
report that:

"My little horse must think it queer
To stop without a farmhouse near
Between the woods and frozen lake
The darkest evening of the year."

Another poet stops differently:

"I have perceived that to be with those I like is enough,
To stop in company with the rest at evening is enough,
To be surrounded by beautiful, curious, breathing,
    laughing flesh is enough."

One cannot imagine Walt Whitman stopping by cold
woods or Robert Frost frolicking amid laughing flesh.[7]
Each has in his own way thickened the meaning he
found in the reality of stopping at day's end and then
incremented that meaning with such exquisite style
that everyone else is stunned by the reality being
revealed with sharp precision, seduced into transacting
more deeply with the real. Thickening meaning and
then incrementing that meaning with style is no easy
task, and it does not happen by accident. It is a
knowledgeable accomplishment of the highest order,
moreso even than what goes on in laboratories, banks,
and institutions of what is called higher learning.
Writing a sonnet is at least as hard as figuring
compound interest or teaching a course, which is why
so few even attempt it.

Sacramental discourse is the same sort of enterprise. It
is not mere garnish to a dull dish of Gospel. Sacrament
is to Gospel what style is to meaning. Christian Gospel

is, like reality itself, larger than any of its sacramental increments, just as redemption is larger than any one of Jesus' own parables about it. But these increments render Gospel operational, effective, gripping, accessible. They thicken Gospel meaning and increment it with style, throwing it open for those to whom it is addressed, saying that it is like a prodigal son come home, a dinner among friends, a swim in the surf.

The Good News, which is what Gospel means, of God's will to commune with a world reconciled to him, even to the point of pouring out his only Son into the strictures of space and time and alienated human malevolence, can never be left as a merely prosaic statement of fact anymore than Frost and Whitman could have left it at saying only that they stopped for the night. Sacramental discourse will bespeak Gospel in ways that embrace and articulate not just words but the whole wordly context in which such a pouring out occurs. It must do this because the Gospel which *sacramentum* images and gives access to is just this all-encompassing. This is why sacramental discourse is primary for understanding the Church, why it transcends and subordinates theological reflection on the Church just as the law of worship transcends and subordinates the law of belief. One cannot know the Church without having access to its paradoxical and inversionary nature, a nature no less paradoxical and inversionary than the fact of a Creator becoming creature, the Source of all becoming the child of an unmarried mother, the impassible submitting to suffering and death. And not to know the Church catholic is not to know the One who has called it into so odd an existence.

There is nothing novel in any of this. It suffuses the various theologies of the patristic period, where it is found focused in and arising from christological concerns addressed in the first several ecumenical councils. These councils were not absorbed with maintaining a Christian platonism but a biblical incarnationalism. The sacramental principle derives from holding that God did in fact become a male of the human species in time and space by the agency of a female of the same species. This makes it inevitable that discourse about the no less human community of believers in him must also unroll in sacramental terms as well.

Christian orthodoxy has rarely if ever talked or acted in terms as exquisitely neat as Richard Niebuhr's Christ against culture, Christ of culture, Christ above culture, and Christ transformer of culture. The tradition has talked and acted more in terms of a God-Man who infests human culture as inmate of it. Only thus could he be transcender, critic, and exorcist of it. He does not transform culture as such. He recreates the World not by making new things but by making all things new. He does this by divine power working upon all that is through the agency of a human nature he holds in solidarity with us. He summons all into a restored communion with his Father, not in spite of matter but through matter, even spit and dirt, thereby clarifying the true meaning of the material world itself. He summons all to his Father in time, thereby renewing both time and its spatial functions. He addresses all people not only in mind and soul but in body as well, thereby renewing the human person in his and her relation to matter, to time and space, and to the whole created world. Apart from this renewal, which is also revelation, we are left as we were—aliens in creation and congenitally alone.

The tradition has never seen the Church as having any purpose or work different from Christ's own. The Church's concerns have always been with the Gospel translated into act, matter, time, and space, with the various cultures the Church has touched being renovated as an inevitable result not directly striven for. Not only is there little conscious reflection on culture as such in the pre-Renaissance Church, but there is surprisingly little *ex professo* writing about the Church itself as distinct from World and City. Thomas Aquinas, certainly one of the greatest theologians of the Church East or West, wrote no self-contained tract on ecclesiology. Rather, what he does say about the Church is almost wholly contained in the third part of his *Summa Theologiae*, which is about the sacraments. It is as though until the modern era, the Church was considered simply as the city center of a restored World, occupied with doing the business of God by faith in Christ. It is now necessary to illustrate what this means in practice.

Chapter Four

Church Doing World

That a major theologian such as Thomas Aquinas
apparently saw no reason to write a self-contained
treatise on the Church, but allowed his ecclesiology to
arise from a rigorous discourse on sacraments, contains
many lessons. One of them seems to be that taking
some things too seriously can result in not taking them
seriously enough.

There is, for example, a way of taking World so
seriously that it is trivialized. People are bombarded
today with the presumption that the worldly worth of a
human existence is determined by the degree to which
the organism is biologically fine-tuned, and that when
the fine-tuning goes out of kilter life in the World
becomes less than worthwhile. The right to a
biologically fine-tuned human existence may then
become an absolute right to good health, an entitlement
over which even the common good cannot prevail. The
common good, in fact, may be reduced to the level of
being servant to the individual's fine-tuned life. Fred's
glands set state policy. This is to take the World so
seriously that it becomes, paradoxically, an expensive
triviality.

Against such a background, Christianity takes World
rather lightly. For if here we have no abiding City, why
should we be concerned with cities and the human
groups—male and female, slave and master, Jew and
Greek, black and white—which inhabit them?

Plundering the community's wealth to pay for fine-tuning the lives of members of such groups seems a massive waste of capital if they must finally die anyhow. Better to put the wealth to more lasting use, into Parthenons and cathedrals whose beauty will nourish millions for centuries rather than into adjusting Fred's glands. Having them adjusted at vast public expense, Fred would nourish few if any, and for relatively no time at all. While it sounds outrageous to say so, Christianity has traditionally been reserved about getting involved with Fred's glands because it does not find them to abide, nor does it find them to be of ultimate significance to many others besides Fred himself. Christianity's sights, it seems, track larger game, and about that larger game Christianity gets very serious indeed.

Similarly with the Church. Ancient theologians are remarkably silent about Church in our modern terms, which is not to say that they do not mention it or concern themselves with it. But their mention of it and their concern with it lie more in the direction of seeing the Church as a function of faith rather than faith as a possible function of a problematic institution. They were more interested and concerned to maintain the churches' peace and faith than in intricate speculation on what the Church might be. The scriptures and tradition had settled all that long since. Augustine, not atypically for theologians of his time of great civil upset and pastoral difficulties, was too preoccupied with being bishop in the church of Hippo to have much time for spinning out ecclesiologies. He did have a towering theology of faith, however, to which his notion of the Church catholic as a communion of churches was subordinated. One can glimpse this in a sermon he preached on Psalm 44:13–14, "The Queen is arrayed in her chamber in robes gold-woven." He said in part: "The apostles preached the word of truth and begot churches not for themselves but for Christ. Behold Rome, behold Carthage, behold all those other cities which became daughters of the king, who delighted in them for his own honor's sake. And all these churches together constitute one Queen Consort of the King . . . one Faith."[8] This most western of church fathers seems to imagine the great churches of his day as a harem of concubines provided by their apostolic progenitors, like lesser sheiks, for the delight of their lord and master, Christ, the sheik of sheiks.

The point I wish to make is that earlier theologians did not ignore the Church any more than healthy people ignore health. But earlier theologians, it seems, did not speak of the Church as we often do today, like hypochondriacs speak of health as an absorbing problem or an absence in their lives. Earlier theologians presume the Church, allude to it, are concerned with it. But their presumptions, allusions, and concern do not suggest pathology or warped obsession so much as the normal taking-for-granted a fish has for water. They could not have imagined, I think, that Christian faith could be lived in any other way than socially, communally, ecclesially, with one foot deep in the scriptures and the other deep in apostolic teaching (*didaskalia*) and fellowship (*koinonia*). They understood the Church to be a holistic enterprise whose faith crisscrossed and interacted with every human experience and institution, rather than a jumble of analytical categories separable from each other and capable of being exploited independently. It seems that they thought it far more important to be Church than to talk a lot about it. In this their approach to the Church exhibits a sort of ruddy good health when compared to our more complex ways of approaching the Church, ways which often seem palsied, nervously abstract, skittish at being too definite, overloaded with disjunctive grammar which freezes the Church in past (bad) or future (good) tenses, and phobic lest it act in a way which might suggest that it savors a triumph at the very heart of its own self-awareness. Our wary approach produces a tentative and propositional shadow of what the Church might be like were it to exist, a vastly qualified committee or therapy group bent to the needs of its members and awash in talk about the vague possibility of doing good somewhere at some time for someone. Such a Church is a far cry from Ignatius of Antioch's declaration that wherever the bishop is, there is the Church Catholic. Ignatius, being on his way to martyrdom in Rome, had little time to fool around.

It seems that we begin by taking the Church too seriously and end by not taking it seriously enough. In view of this, it may help to realize that in order to learn how earlier Christians really understood Church as well as World, we cannot look only at polemical works, conciliar definitions, or at later tractates *de ecclesia*. One might look first of all at the sacramental discourse of articulated enactments by which earlier Christians corporately set about doing the World in the presence of the World's Creator. This is strange territory for us moderns since it will amount to an examination not only of words but of events as well, events which incorporate words without being reduced to them. These events are those of liturgical worship, which punctuates Christian communal life with regular frequency from earliest times. Perhaps from such an examination a holistic ecclesiology may emerge, at least in an outline accessible to modern minds.

To begin with, one must not forget that Judaism and Christianity have traditionally set the highest store on divine worship. In fact, most Jews and Christians have for thousands of years expressed their religious existence not in books but by participation in assemblies which have met regularly, at least once a week, for worship of the living God. The ordinary, normal Jew or Christian need not be theologically literate or possess a theological degree, and it would surely strike them as odd to suggest that gaining such a degree is somehow more important than the Kiddush meal on Sabbath or Mass on Sunday. In saying this, my intention is not to insinuate some particular view on the nature of religion, but only to observe the fact that Jews and Christians have tended to gather for, and set great store by, worship on certain regularly recurring days, usually the last or the first days of that peculiar unit of time we call the week.[9]

Christians have from earliest times assembled for worship on the first day of the week, a day called *kyriake*, Lord's Day. By reorganizing the week so as to have it culminate on the first rather than the last day, as in Judaism, early Christians not only established a day which commemorated Jesus' historical resurrection from the dead but tapped into, not the Sabbath, but into the old Jewish eschatological symbolism of the "Eighth Day"—the span of time following the completion of creation in redemption accomplished by the Messiah. Christians rapidly gave the Lord's Day, Sunday, a definite structure which became more detailed and elaborate as the lives of believers organized themselves in communal form, a structure which would become the paradigm for other days of assembly, or feasts, falling during the week. By the fifth century, Sunday and festal worship in major churches such as those of Jerusalem, Antioch, Alexandria, Rome, and the new Christian city of Constantinople had already come to be not a single service, as we are used to today, but an interlocking series of services which gave form not only to the day itself but to the entire week, the year, and time itself.

Preaching could and did occur at almost any point in the sequence of services. John Chrysostom preached his great series of sermons on Genesis toward day's end, before evening prayer or vespers. In some Palestinian churches, moreover, not only the bishop preached at the eucharistic service, but all his assisting senior clergy preached after him in sequence. The sermon, indeed, became almost a service in its own right and might take up a considerable amount of time: Chrysostom sometimes preached for over two hours as his hearers wept, cheered, pounded their breasts, and applauded.

The time-scale of this entire series of services was the whole of a Sunday. The space-scale of it was the whole city. The time consumed by all these worship events may have been six to eight hours, not counting intervals between the various events. No doubt relatively few people attended them all, nor do they appear to have been expected to do so. One attended however much one's ability, piety, and health permitted. The ill, infirm, and elderly probably attended much shorter versions of the city's full liturgy in their small neighborhood chapel or church. It seems that the full public liturgy of the city was thus not designed primarily for parochial needs, nor does it appear to have catered to congregations. Rather, this full public liturgy, this urban act, this duty owed to God like taxes were owed to the state (the word *leitourgia* was used in antiquity to designate both sorts of acts) was simply the Church manifested in its deepest nature in the human *civitas* as the presence, the embodiment in the world of the World to come, of the Kingdom, of the new and final age. It was the Church of Jesus Christ being most overtly itself before God in the world on humanity's urban stage. Its structure might consist in as many as seven related but distinct services.

The first service occurred, as in the synagogue, with psalms of praise (*laudes*) around daybreak, when business began in the world of the time.

The second service consisted in the gradual assemblage, around early or midmorning, of clergy and people at a designated place (*statio*) in some city neighborhood or open space large enough to accommodate large numbers of people. After prayer and reading from the Bible, the group set off in procession, accompanied by psalmody, to the church designated for the day, probably picking up other people as the procession wound its way through the streets, pausing here and there for rest, prayer, and more readings from the Bible. When the designated, or "stational," church was reached, the whole procession, clergy and people, entered it in state, singing psalms of entry.

By late morning or midday, a third service, this time that of the Word, began in the stational church. This included anywhere from two to five scriptural readings interspersed with psalms of meditation and concluding with reading from a gospel and perhaps a homily by the presiding minister, normally the bishop of the city.

After this a fourth service of petitionary prayers, together with dismissals of the unbaptized, penitents, and certain others took place. So extensive was this process of dismissing with prayer those who were not considered capable of offering the eucharistic sacrifice of praise and thanksgiving, and so important a pastoral office was this process considered to be, that it came to give its name, *missa*, not only to the entire eucharistic service itself but also to parts of the liturgy of the hours, which ended with similar petitionary prayers and the dismissal of the whole assembly. In the stational liturgy, these prayers usually took either a bidding form (a summons to prayer, silent prayer by all, a summary prayer by the presiding minister, and a dismissal), as at Rome, or a litanic form (brief petitions announced by a deacon and responded to with *kyrie eleison* by the assembly), as in the East. These prayers for those being dismissed were then continued into a lengthy series of petitions by the remaining baptized faithful for the world, the City, and the Church particular and universal. Only after so solemn a series of prayers was it thought appropriate that the kiss of peace could be exchanged as a sign of the assembly's reconciliation with God and of the church's baptized members with each other. This extensive service of petitionary prayers thus constituted not a "penitential office," but an office of reconciliation without which it was not considered possible for the assembly to proceed to the eucharistic banquet. After the old Roman dismissals fell into disuse and the Prayers of the Faithful faded, Gregory the Great (+604) seems to have made the reconciling prayer of the Roman *missa* the Our Father, which he inserted during the preparation for communion and concluded with the kiss of peace. Here it still stands, now compromised by a "penitential office" concluding with an absolution at the beginning of the Word service.

By this time it was afternoon, and bread and wine were brought to the altar table in a procession accompanied by psalmody and increasingly elaborate ceremonial in larger churches. Like any parade, this took time to organize and was often a rather rowdy affair of considerable proportions.[10] The bringing of the gifts of bread, water, and wine to the table by deacons is already mentioned by Justin around 150. In 1961 I witnessed a papal liturgy on Good Friday in which the procession to bring the presanctified gifts to the altar of St. Mary Major from the sacrament chapel took over an hour, developing a scale which turned the procession into a service in its own right.

Once the gifts were arranged on the table, the bishop, surrounded by his clergy, prayed over them at some length and then distributed communion until all had participated in both bread and cup. This also must have become a lengthy process as major city churches grew to hold thousands of communicants. By the time this was finished, perhaps even after the senior clergy had cleaned up and gone home, it was midafternoon or later.

The day concluded before sundown, when all business ceased, with a seventh and final service of lamp-lighting (*lucernarium*) and hymnic psalmody, or vespers.

Perhaps this generalized scheme of Christian community worship as it emerged in an urban frame will be enough to suggest some areas for pastoral and theological reflection. We today can hardly be expected to understand how liturgy could be considered seriously as the basic condition for doing theology, even less as the law which founds or constitutes the law of belief, so long as we perceive liturgical worship as a pastel endeavor shrunk to only forty-five minutes and consisting of some organ music, a choral offering, a few lines of scripture, a short talk on religion, a collection, and perhaps a quick consumption of disks or pellets and a beverage.

Worship in earlier days was richer and of vaster scale. It unfolded throughout the day and throughout the city, even when many neighborhoods in the old cities of paganism no doubt remained hostile to the Christian presence. In such contexts, the sort of urban liturgy described above would have had an unavoidable evangelical function. Its hymnal was the psalter, its texts almost exclusively scripture, its musical instrument the human voice, its agent the whole city, its purpose to serve a restored creation given iconic form in civil artifacts which, together, were regarded as the highest achievement of humanity, creation's servant. Its participants over time, from Sunday to Sunday, from feast to feast, from year to year, would have found themselves steeped in God's Word proclaimed, heard, preached, sung, and celebrated to an extent we find difficult to imagine today. In terms of sheer quantity, of sheer time spent in public proximity to God and prayer and worship, most modern Christians who are thought to be normally observant rarely would engage in this much worship over the course of several months, if then.

And when they do so, the ethos of their worship is quite different. Rather than worshipping publicly in their own name, they more often than not worship in public by following, individually, printed texts composed by others and used by ordained professionals who enact the worship event in their presence and in their name.[11] Given this, the notion that this privatized and vicarious act, done entirely in one place before a seated audience, has any implications for or connection with the human City in which it occurs, or that it has any roots in or effect upon the *res publica* of Church and World, is hard to take seriously. The pastoral and theological results of so severe a constriction of experience, reflection, stimulation, imagination, and enactment upon the awareness of Christian communities and individuals are as far-reaching as they should be disturbing. It is as though the Church has suffered a hemorrhage in its central nervous system, a stroke which has deadened its senses and paralyzed its ability to move as it must and express itself as it is expected to do. Having become significantly dysfunctional, the Church is then quietly spun off to the periphery of the World, evacuating the World's urban center of all witness to the true ends for which both World and human City exist. A palsied Church finds itself sitting beside the City's deathbed, mumbling words of comfort in the eye of the storm.

Neurologists point out that a human being, so far from being born with innate coordination of its senses, must grow itself into a sort of envelope of sensation which then forms for the individual his or her own peculiar physical and emotional self-image. An infant first regards its limbs as strangers. Only by constant and long-term stimulation does the child come to recognize its own members as part of itself. It learns to associate pain and other sensations with various bodily parts, even to the point that should the individual lose an arm or leg the limb's sensations continue to be identified in the now empty space the limb used to occupy. It seems that an individual's nervous system creates and holds in being that individual's real self-image and awareness of a personal identity which is the individual's fundamental principle of operation.

Analogously, a corporate entity such as a church might perhaps be said to grow itself into a sort of envelope of sensation which then forms its own peculiar self-image, its own real awareness of corporate identity which is its own fundamental principle of operation. The stimulation process which is most responsible for a church's growth into its own identity-envelope, and which is therefore responsible as well for how that church functions in the real order, is its life of constant and increasingly complex worship. For in worship alone is the church gathered in the closest obvious proximity to its fundamental values, values which are always assuming stimulative form in time, space, image, word, and repeated act. The richer this stimulation is, under the criteria of the Gospel, it follows that the more conscious, aware, self-possessed, and vigorously operational the given church will be.

And to the extent that the analogy with sensate growth in individuals is valid, the obverse must be true as well. An unstimulated or understimulated church will bear certain resemblances to an unstimulated or understimulated human being. Such people develop weak or warped superegos which break down or become recessive under stress, even rendering the individual dysfunctional at times. Such a church develops markedly weak or warped senses of its own identity and witness, senses which may break down or become recessive under stress, even rendering the church dysfunctional at times. The church then may begin to dissemble its nature and function, becoming a commune of friends whose main purpose is to get along with each other, a moral uplift society, a group dedicated to aesthetics or therapy, a sheepfold of the unsure, a home for the dull.

The great civil liturgy schematized above must have had a profound stimulatory effect on the ancient urban churches which evolved and employed it many times each year for centuries, to end only when the cities themselves were destroyed and their populace dispersed. It compares to what many modern Christians know as worship like the Ring Series of Wagner compares to a ballad, like Beowulf compares to a television jingle, like the ceiling of the Sistine Chapel compares to a billboard. Whatever else such a civil liturgy may have done to those who knew and took part in it, it seems to have given them a certain robust self-confidence in owning their Christian faith as it faced challenges such as the collapse of western civilization and the creation of new cultures. It pulled them together in all their urban diversity to focus on making a World after the mind of God in Christ. It did not separate them out into exclusivist ghettos concerned with consolation, passivity, and self-therapy.

I would not argue that this sort of liturgical engagement was a wholly novel act of Christian genius. The ancient Mediterranean world's notions about politics and the state rested largely upon the traditions of urban society; the first states were cities and were constrained by the scale of urban politics at least in Greece and, later, Rome. For all its far-flung boundaries, the later Roman empire remained an extension of the city itself. Christianity did not invent any of this, but inherited it as the only evangelical, liturgical, and theological paradigm at hand for pulling its diversities together and getting on with its mission. And as it would never have occurred to a Greek, a Roman, or even a Jewish citizen of Athens, Rome, or Jerusalem that a city could be without its own proper cult, so too it seems that the same assumption was shared by contemporary Christians. After his conversion to Christ, Constantine attempted to alter the ancient cult of Rome by insinuating Christian places of worship into the ceremonial center of the city. The old pagan establishment successfully resisted this attempt, forcing the emperor to build his churches only in Rome's suburbs—which is why to this day the great churches of Rome, such as St. Peter's, St. Paul's, St. John Lateran and others lie at some distance from the Forum in neighborhoods which were originally suburban. His failure to penetrate the cultic center of Rome for Christianity may indeed have been one reason, among others, why Constantine would found a new capital which could be characterized as a totally Christian city with Christian monuments forming its ceremonial center: Constantinople.[12]

Christians after Constantine would have had to improvise in Old Rome rather differently from those in New Rome. The complete Christianization of Rome was slower than the Christianization of Constantinople. The many pagan temples of Rome were not finally secularized until 408, barely two years before the first sack of the city by barbarians in 410, an event which caused an outcry that the disaster was linked to Rome's having forsaken its old gods and their cult. Augustine in North Africa wrote *Civitas Dei* to disprove the allegations.

The evolution of Roman urban liturgy was affected by all this. It was based on the scattering of churches around the suburbs which could hold large congregations. Until well after the Renaissance, the bishop's cathedral, St. John Lateran, still lay apart from the inhabited part of the city. To attend the Pope's liturgy in his own church, Romans would have had to walk or drive a considerable distance out of town. Moreover, the old neighborhood churches (*tituli*) which finally grew up in the city center tended to be small due to urban crowding and thus incapable of accommodating large gatherings. So too were the social service centers (*diaconiae*) with their chapels. The only large liturgical spaces were to be found in the bishop's churches and in the great basilicas erected in cemeteries to honor major Roman martyrs such as Peter, Paul, Sebastian, and Lawrence, and all of these large churches were suburban or exurban.

The need to penetrate the city center with moving groups of Christians in order to proclaim the new faith in a worshipful manner must therefore have been one concern which gave rise to Roman worship on the town, so to speak. It was one way to renovate and Christianize the old cult of the *urbs Romae* despite lingering hostility in many neighborhoods and enormous logistical problems. Following Ignatius of Antioch's dictum that where the bishop is there is the Church Catholic, the bishop of Rome moved around the city presiding at services which strove, whether in large or small spaces, to manifest and celebrate the Church's full nature and scope.[13] Such processional activity, undertaken to weld the city to a common cult, was common in pagan times both in Rome and elsewhere. Christians simply took up the practice in order to suffuse the old city with a new cult developed around the Good News of God's pleasure for the World in Christ. They met old tradition not by sidestepping it or creating a new tradition which would oppose the old, but by penetrating the older tradition of urban worship and filling it with new meaning. In doing so they found it possible to make use of many of the old institutions in new ways. The old orders of pagan priesthood could be transformed into new orders of Christian service; the old chief priest of paganism, the Pontifex Maximus, became the bishop of the city; the people, who had mainly watched the old pagan worship services of sacrifice from afar, now found themselves brought right into the new Christian temples as active participants in the new worship. As the Church retained old familiar urban structures, it also used them to effect a significant and far-reaching egalitarian revolution in Roman society, a revolution which raised the lower classes to a degree of enfranchisement in the supreme cultic act of the city they had never attained before, and lowered the upper classes to the level of being "servants of the servants of God." Pagan apologists perceived this revolution early on, expressing their dismay at its egalitarian trends in its barnlike architecture and in its use of inelegant popular language even for religious discourse. They played the same tune as the British military band at the surrender at Yorktown: "The World Turned Upside Down."

That all this happened as the result of Christian hubris, inadvertence, or apostasy from the pure Gospel is an opinion which only ignorance can support. The liturgical evidence alone suggests that it was a quite knowledgeable accomplishment undertaken to bespeak the faith of Christians in ways accessible to entire urban populations at the time. It was not as though Christian worship was being adapted to pagan cultures, but the contrary. Pagan cultures, which reached their greatest systemizations in and around the great urban centers of the ancient world, were being slowly, carefully adapted to a new vision carried by a new people who did old things in a new way. The entire process obviously stimulated the old culture. But it perhaps stimulated the new people even more, deepening their memories, expanding their minds, causing them to recognize new relationships between their religious stance and the world at large. It probably did not make them any more one, holy, or apostolic than their Christian ancestors, but it did enlarge their sense of what it was to be catholic, a word derived from the Greek *kata holos*, meaning whole, entire, and meant for all. Urban liturgy was, it seems, the anvil on which this was being pounded out with the help and participation of all sorts and conditions of Christians at the time, for they corporately were, and remain, the agent of the liturgical act. And what they shape is not mere ceremony. It is an enacted ecclesiology, a realized eschatology; a theology, in short, which is constitutive and fundamental for the ways in which faith looks upon the World and the human City.

Yet all this can be reduced to an apologetic argument for the liturgy to be taken seriously because of its value in utilitarian terms. I wish to maintain that Christian worship does not stop with merely stimulating the community of believers. Nor does the stimulation of the community merely aid it to be itself and do its job. I think that when the Church enters into a context of worship as complex and grand as that described heretofore—one worthy of Creation and congruent with the human City within which the Church abides as witness to its singular reconciliation to God in

Christ—then something vastly mysterious transpires in the Church itself. While this will be difficult to put into words, we will attempt something of it in the next four chapters. Meanwhile, it may help to review where we have been.

We set out from the halls of academe, gusty with talk about talk, where one may spend one's life training tour guides to take suburbanites on fast trips into the inner City. We noted that the trip had to pass through strip-cities filled with stores selling cheap fixes, dubious cosmologies, and junk food, occasionally displaying freaks in cages for our amusement. These cities were not part of the original landscape, but were built there by us who found raw nature too fraught with implications we preferred to ignore. Then we drove fast through the inner City, where money and social recipes littered empty streets lined by massage parlors and butcher shops displaying goods no sane tourist would touch. We deplored it all, but the deploring seasoned nicely our return home to the suburbs where things were at least neat, the lawns mowed, the tube still warm, and our blessings stood bright and shiny in the medicine cabinet waiting to be counted once again. We could attend our neighborhood church to be soothed in the knowledge that all was well as our tour guide slipped into leotards to dance, yet again, an interpretation of the Twenty-third Psalm.

I suggested that this is not a cure for *Weltschmerz* but its cause; that it had to do with our having accepted not the World at face value but ourselves as all there really is. Having accepted that, it was inexorable that I was free to say the same thing about you: that I am all that is or matters. I then found speech unnecessary, society expendable, the inner city a bad dream, the Church a vaguely consoling fraud, God rather less than an option, politics futile, art what I like, and anomie all that was left. I rediscovered how comfortable the fetal position could really be. And with that I sank quietly from sight; a video game in one hand, a bottle in the other, all my problems effectively solved.

By suggesting this, I hoped to set up a situation in which alternatives might stand out in high contrast— such as World, City, and Church as artifacts, as things we make. I tried to seduce us all into artistic discourse, into talking and thinking about how we make and, in making, discover reality. If we could grow ourselves into that discovered reality, I suggested, we might stumble onto the road out of suburbia, a road best traveled not in a tour bus but on foot so that we could stop when we wished in cold woods, with laughing flesh, to admire ladies in silk dresses and their beaux, and even get ourselves swept up into a rowdy mob on its way downtown to do the world now and then, there perhaps to encounter a new possibility leaning into the wind.

That such a new possibility might be a view of liturgical worship as a constitutive and foundational theological enterprise is something we might now investigate.

Liturgy and Theology

Chapter Five

Liturgical Theology

Two questions immediately plague one who sets off in
search of liturgical theology. The first is the question,
what is liturgy? The second is then, in that case, what is
theology? Both liturgy and theology are highly
equivocal terms today. Liturgy is applied to almost any
ceremonialized human gathering, sacred or secular.
Theology has come to designate almost any sort of
religious discourse, in particular those arguments one
wishes to denigrate as being hopelessly ideological and
thus out of touch with reality, as when it is said that
Reaganomics is "theological." In view of all this it may
be well to begin by dwelling on what theology is,
especially when it is modified by the adjective
"liturgical."

Urban Holmes once noted that good liturgy borders on
the vulgar. He also said that liturgy leads regularly to
the edge of chaos, and that from this regular flirt with
doom comes a theology different from any other.[14] So
phrased, the observation bears all the marks of a great
truth: it is obscure, profound, sweeping, and infects
one with a cerebral itch which compels one to scratch
up insights of various kinds. One such insight is that
"theology" is not the very first result of an assembly's
being brought by liturgical experience to the edge of
chaos. Rather, it seems that what results in the first
instance from such an experience is deep change in the
very lives of those who participate in the liturgical act.
And deep change will affect their next liturgical act,

73

howsoever slightly. To detect that change in the subsequent liturgical act will be to discover where theology has passed, rather as physics detects atomic particles in tracks of their passage through a liquid medium.

There is nothing placid or genteel about either process. In each there is collision, chaos, and a certain violence. In the liturgical instance, what has happened is an adjustment in the assembly of participants to its having been brought to the brink of chaos in the previous liturgical act. This adjustment causes the next liturgical act to be in some degree different from its predecessor because those who do the next act have been unalterably changed. The adjustment to change between acts on the part of the actors is both conscious and unconscious; it is always real. The results of this adjustment show in the gradual evolution of the liturgical rites themselves. This is how liturgies grow. Their growth is a function of adjustment to deep change caused in the assembly by its being brought regularly to the brink of chaos in the presence of the living God. It is the *adjustment* which is theological in all this. I hold that it is theology being born, theology in the first instance. It is what tradition has called *theologia prima.*

For many this puts us on strange ground indeed, for since the high Middle Ages with the advent of the university and of scientific method, we have become accustomed to the notion that theology is something done in academies out of books by elites with degrees producing theologies of this and that. Theological curricula are filled with such efforts.[15] To argue with minds accustomed to thinking of theology in such a manner that theology at its genesis is communitarian, even proletarian; that it is aboriginally liturgical in context, partly conscious and partly unconscious; that it stems from an experience of near chaos; that it is long term and dialectical; and that its agents are more likely to be charwomen and shopkeepers than pontiffs and professors—all this is to argue against the grain. It is to argue that the theology which we most readily recognize and practice is in fact neither primary nor seminal but secondary and derivative: *theologia secunda.* It is also to argue that doing liturgical theology comes closer to doing *theologia prima* than *theologia secunda* or a "theology of the liturgy," and that doing primary theology places a whole set of requirements on the theologian which are not quite the same as those placed on a theologian who does only secondary theology.

For what emerges most directly from an assembly's liturgical act is not a new species of theology among others. It is *theologia* itself. Nor is it inchoate and raw, despite the fact that it is always open to endless further specification and exploitation by human minds. This may be the reason why Alexander Schmemann wrote that the liturgy " . . . is not an 'authority' or a *locus theologicus*; it is the ontological condition of theology, of the proper understanding of *kerygma*, of the Word of God, because it is in the Church, of which the *leitourgia* is the expression and the life, that the sources of theology are functioning precisely as sources."[16] Schmemann's observation stresses the articulated intimacy which locks the liturgy into the church which does the liturgy, noting that the liturgy is not some thing separate from the church, but simply the church caught in the act of being most overtly itself as it stands faithfully in the presence of the One who is both object and source of that faith. The liturgical assembly's stance in faith is vertiginous, on the edge of chaos. Only grace and favor enable it to stand there; only grace and promise brought it there; only grace and a rigorous divine charity permit the assembly, like Moses, to come away whole from such an encounter, and even then it is with wounds which are as deep as they are salutary.

Here is where "something vastly mysterious" transpires in the Church as it engages in worship worthy of Creation and congruent with the human City within which it abides as witness to God in Christ. As Leo the Great said, those things which were conspicuous in the life of our Redeemer here pass over into the *sacramenta*, into the worship of the Church—agreeing, I think, with Holmes and Schmemann. The worshipping assembly never comes away from such an experience unchanged, and the assembly's continuing adjustment to that change is not merely a theological datum but theology itself. Theology on this primordial level is thus a sustained dialectic. Its *thesis* is the assembly as it enters into the liturgical act; its *antithesis* is the assembly's changed condition as it comes away from its liturgical encounter with the living God in Word and sacrament; its *synthesis* is the assembly's adjustment in faith and works to that encounter. The adjustment comprises whole sets of acts both great and small, conscious and unconscious, all of which add up to a necessarily critical and reflective theology which is architectonic for the content and significance of the assembly's address to reality itself—both inside and outside church, on the first day and throughout all other days of the week as well.

These perceptions can perhaps be confirmed by anyone who is an experienced and astute participator in Christian liturgical worship. As for myself, I have witnessed all this happening in a fairly regular way during forty years of participation in liturgical acts of every kind in various Rites all over the world, East as well as West. One learns to recognize the signals an assembly of faithful people gives off when, in a liturgical event, it begins to change palpably into something it was not when the event began. These signals are not wholly dissimilar from those given off by people involved in a great act of making music. Yet the liturgical change is clearly not an aesthetic one at base, for what catalyzes such change cannot be said to be merely an act of art. It is something more, and it happens unpredictably, as often as not in spite of the art or artlessness of the given liturgical event. I have known it to happen in the middle of a thoroughly bad sermon and at the end of a good one, in baroque pontifical Masses and in helter-skelter baptisms in basements. In St. Mary Major on Good Friday and in a small oratory in Indiana on a ferial Wednesday. During the reading of the martyrology at prime in a monastery and during Benediction of the Blessed Sacrament on a hillside in Tennessee. I have felt its centuries-old residue in empty churches from Canterbury to Hong Kong. It almost always happens stunningly at funerals. But it always happens to some extent as the daily fare of those who have received and live by the promise of One who said "I am with you always."

From perceptions such as these, I infer that the adjustment which the assembly undertakes in response to the God-induced change it suffers in its liturgical events is a dynamic, critical, reflective, and sustained act of theology in the first instance, of *theologia prima*. And I maintain that our fall from this into *theologia secunda* has imperceptibly rendered us aphasic and inept in regard to it. For this reason, it is far easier for us to write and react to theologies *of* the liturgy than to perceive liturgical theology as it occurs and factor its results wisely for the life of the world.

Our aphasic ineptitude with liturgical theology as *theologia prima* may also be why our pastoral theology is often so remotely pastoral and so genially untheological, quite unlike the theology practiced by the Church fathers, a theology which was with few exceptions thoroughly pastoral. It was a theology preached from within or in close connection with the liturgy rather than taught systematically in classrooms. And, finally, our aphasia concerning *theologia prima* seems to be the reason why we struggle so hard for such modest results in our ecumenical dialogues with certain Eastern Christian churches in which *theologia prima* remains the basic way of doing theology. They speak primary theology to us, we speak secondary theology to them, and we both slide past each other making cordial gestures which are finally equivocal.

I cite these instances to suggest only something of the nature of primary theology by calling attention to some of the warps its absence throws into the entire theological enterprise. For if theology as a whole is critical reflection upon the communion between God and our race, the peculiarly graced representative and servant of cosmic order created by God and restored in Christ, then scrutiny of the precise point at which this communion is most overtly deliberated upon and celebrated by us under God's judgment and in God's presence would seem to be crucial to the whole enterprise. If this be true, then the *professional* liturgical theologian, whose task is to articulate foundational faith as fully as possible and relate it to the array of secondary theological disciplines, bears a heavy responsibility both to his or her colleagues in worship and to *theologia secunda* in all its aspects. Massey Shepherd said as much to the North American Academy of Liturgy in 1978. "If we believe," he said, "that worship is the experiential foundation of theological reflection, that the practice of worship is the source of rubrical and canonical legislation, and that the ministry of clergy and laity is exhibited most clearly in liturgical assemblies, then it is incumbent upon our Academy to work for this recognition. It is the unfortunate way of our Western tradition to compartmentalize particular concerns in separate consultations and commissions that need to be coordinated. It is not enough to publish position papers or send resolutions to ecclesiastical authorities."[17]

I am not sure that the professionals in the Academy entirely comprehended what a large task Shepherd's words called them to. The task appears to be the same one which the words of Holmes, Schmemann, and Leo the Great imply. The thrust of Shepherd's words pushes the task of the professional liturgical theologian toward inquiry into the fundamental nature of a liturgical act itself. Note that I do not say the fundamental nature of liturgy in general, but a liturgical act itself. For liturgy in general is a convenient abstraction, a category we use to signal vastly differentiated sets of motives, acts, and patterns. Like all such categorical abstractions, liturgy in general is so fascinating in its very generality that as it excites it also blinds and leads one astray. The fact is that liturgy in general does not exist in the real order. It is a mental construct, an analogical spread; like all analogies, it is capable of obscuring real differences by the splendor of the sameness it provides without toil or hazard for those whose inclination is to avoid the toil of getting their facts straight and to avoid the hazard of being discovered to have been wrong. Such people excel in making obvious generalizations which may well be destructive when reduced to practice. But when one approaches a concrete liturgical event, or an actual tradition of such events, one needs first to place tempting analogies well after the toil of discriminating facts and accounting for differences. One must also learn quickly to hazard being wrong and be prepared to change one's mind. Liturgy, like language, is not always logical, and one who begins to learn one language by studying language in general begins badly.

In this connection one might notice what Lévi-Strauss calls the surface structure of a specific language system, and compare it to a specific liturgical system.[18] Even an

untrained observer can tell the obvious differences
between French and English, between a Byzantine
Divine Liturgy and a Methodist Covenant Service. It
takes greater discipline, however, to go deeper into the
surface structure. One must learn new vocabulary,
alien grammar, different syntax in both language and
liturgy. One must also unlearn the ways one has
spoken and worshipped before if one is ever to
experience the other idiom from the inside, so to speak,
as it is experienced by its natives, and this is yet more
difficult to do. But it takes an even greater degree of
discipline, which comes only with years of constant
effort, before one can move beneath the surface into the
deep structure of a language, of a mythic corpus, or of a
given liturgical system. Here alone one begins to
discover commonality, and commonality is the
foundation for all generalization, the prerequisite of all
system.[19]

It is only at this level that one begins to detect certain
common laws according to which linguistic, mythic,
and liturgical systems function. But while the
structuralist may be seeking meaning, Robert Taft
thinks that the more immediate chore for the
professional liturgical theologian is to seek the liturgical
structure itself. "For in the history of liturgical
development," he points out, "structure outlives
meaning. Elements are preserved even when their
meaning is lost . . . , or when they have become
detached from their original limited place and purpose,
acquiring new and broader meanings in the process.
And elements are introduced which have no apparent
relationship to others." He goes on to observe that in
the history of liturgical *explanation* there has been a
contrary shift from structure to interpretation.
Beginning in the Middle Ages, commentators attended
more to the "symbolic" meaning of the various
liturgical units, and their interpretations often did

violence to structure. In the sixteenth century, these interpretations took on a particular theological and polemical cast among both Reformers and Catholics, a step which led quickly to a secondary theology officially defined as "correct" now determining rather than interpreting liturgical text and form.[20]

The step was momentous because it confirmed many on both sides of the schism in a notion of *orthodoxia* not as a sustained life of "right worship," but as "correct doctrine" to be maintained by centralized ecclesiastical authority having exclusive power to enforce an absolute standard in liturgical texts by law. This was something unheard of in western Christianity prior to the English Act of Uniformity of 1549, the direct effect of which was to establish as the only liturgy allowed in England that contained in *The Booke of the Common Prayer and Administration of the Sacraments, and other Rites and Ceremonies of the Church, after the use of the Churche of England*. Similar steps were not begun by the Roman See until years later, during the Council of Trent, and not even finished initially until 1614.

But if the policy originated in England, Rome took it to the farthest limits. One can see this happening in the fate of one phrase in the Roman Canon's *Te igitur* prayer. This prayer, which antedates its first appearance in the Gelasian Sacramentary of the eighth century, mentions the Pope and the local bishop and then concludes with the phrase, added perhaps by Alcuin in the ninth century: *et omnibus orthodoxis atque catholicae et apostolicae fidei cultoribus*. A literal translation of the liturgically traditional Latin might read: "and with all right-worshipping cultivators of catholic and apostolic faith." Yet an imprimatured English translation of 1961 makes this read: "and for all those right-believing teachers who have the guardianship of the catholic and apostolic faith,"[21] a considerable secondary theological paraphrase. Even after the

Second Vatican Council, the official English rendering maintains this: "and for all those who hold and teach the catholic faith that comes to us from the apostles."

Orthodoxia, right worship, in both translations and in the mentality which produced them, has become *orthopistis*, right believing, or *orthodidascalia*, right teaching, and both are by the context centered upon church officials. Right worship was ceasing to be the ontological condition of theology, of the proper understanding of the proclaimed Word of God, becoming instead a *locus theologicus* in service to correct belief and teaching by church officials and secondary theologians, who were using the liturgy as a quarry for stones to set into arguments shaped by increasingly rigorous methodologies worked out in academe.[22] The antithesis of orthodoxy has become heresy rather than heterodoxy, "wrong worship." Praxis and belief have grown apart.

The gains achieved by this are undeniable and they affect us all, in many instances for the better. But the bills we must pay for these gains are calculated infrequently and they are high. As secondary theology moves farther away from the primary theological enterprise of right worship or *orthodoxia*, and as that move becomes a divorce on grounds of incompatibility due to modern academic method and structure, several mutations occur. Ministry changes from consecrated service to communities of faith into first a profession, then a trade, and finally into an avocation for some and a series of options for others. Homiletics becomes less the hearing of the gospel out loud, so to speak, among one's peers in faith than an occasion for the certified to educate the uncertified about "issues" through argumentation, syllabi, and oratorical tricks. Sacraments diminish as unsettling encounters between living presences divine and human in the here and now, to become a rather abstract ritual expression of a pattern set by Christ to give scope to the universal Kingdom.[23] Second order doctrinal language begins to take priority over the first order language of *leitourgia* and forces it into discourses which are usually carried on quite apart from doctrine—discourses such as the aesthetic, the ethical, the educational, and those of self-fulfillment and self-expression. The liturgy may be viewed as rather important, but mainly to the extent that it discharges a role of keeping a sense of Christian values alive in the community and remains an effective vehicle of transmitting the Christian vision of the Kingdom.[24]

At this point our access to the now receding matter of *theologia prima* and the milieu of *orthodoxia* out of which that theology arises becomes increasingly problematical, and our grasp on liturgy itself begins to slip. The liturgy no longer serves as the constitutive foundation for secondary theology, but is reduced to a doxological *envoi* which concludes the secondary enterprise and is wholly controlled by it.[25] *Lex supplicandi legem statuat credendi* is effectively reversed, with the law of belief founding and constituting the law of worship. Furthermore the liturgical assembly, which has been meeting under God fifty-two times a year for the past 2,000, now must be regarded as a theological cipher drawing whatever theological awareness it has not from its own response to its graced encounter with the living God, but from sources found in ecclesiastical bureaucracies and within the walls of academe. The served has become servant, mistress has become handmaid.

We thus find ourselves affirming brave new things which fly in the face of common human experience, being unable to perceive or account for whole ranges of data which cannot be fitted into the new paradigm. Our position on doctrine's control over worship, for example, is similar to someone in linguistics maintaining that language is controlled by philologists rather than by the social transaction which is the act of speech itself—an act which is coterminous with the origin of human society and continuously constituting that society as a continuum of meaningful discourse between its members.

Philologists do not set the laws which permit language. They study its acts as formalized in words. Editors do not create language. They arrange its acts as formalized in words. Philosophers do not originate language. They formulate intelligibility tests to clarify and bring greater precision to the implications of its acts as formalized in concepts and words. All three of these honorable activities represent not first but second order enterprises. It was, after all, not Aristotle who spoke the first word, but some nameless creature we today might be hard pressed to identify as human. We would, moreover, probably have even greater difficulty in understanding that at that very same point human society—that sustained mutuality of complex relationships made possible precisely by language— had begun to exist. And when speech and society began to exist, all the arts took their inception as well: music in the first word's pitch and tone; politics in the mutual relationships which both caused and were enabled by the first word; crafts in the common needs to which those relationships gave rise; and all the arts we call fine in the symbolic ambiguity of the first word, an ambiguity which lifted it entirely beyond the static precision of the first bark of the first dog.

All this might suggest to us that the effect of doctrine upon liturgy, like the effect of philology upon language, is a truth but not the whole truth. It might also suggest to us that liturgy and language have more in common with each other than either of them have with doctrine and philology. Language is correlative with human society rather as liturgy is correlative with Church; in each, language and liturgy are both constitutive and constituted as enterprises of the first order. And it is helpful to remember in this connection that the human agents of first order enterprises such as liturgy and language are usually anonymous. We do not know who spoke the first word or sang the first poem any more than we know who first spoke any of the words on this page, despite the fact that whoever did any of these things achieved quite major accomplishments. Nor do we know who presided at the first eucharist after the Last Supper, or when; or who first prayed the old Roman *canon missae* either in its Milanese or in its Roman form; or who first sang *sanctus* at Mass; or who moved the Byzantine *prothesis* to its present position before the Divine Liturgy; or who composed almost any ancient liturgical text or originated almost any ceremonial gesture one might care to name. The point is that in first order matters, anonymity is the rule, intentions are obscure, and meaning is less precise than it is richly ambiguous.

To resolve anonymity, determine intention, and bring precision in first order matters is usually frustrating. It is also to miss the point of what is important. What seems to be of fundamental importance in first order matters is to understand something of how a given liturgical act or act of language reveals some crucial aspect of a church's or a society's whole continuum of discourse, and how the act affects and is affected by that same continuum. To understand something of these things is to know how all human societies function by learning how one human society has functioned or still functions. It is not merely to learn about old texts, but to learn how and why they were produced and what they produce. What they produce is, among other things, ourselves. How they produced us is therefore a matter of uncommon interest.

One might, for example, set out to learn how *Beowulf*, an act of language, reveals some crucial aspect of Saxon society's continuum of discourse—affecting it and being affected by it, constituting it and giving it peculiar shape.[26] This would involve one in more than just seeking what the poem "means." It is to learn how the poem "works" in and from its social context, and how all acts of language (matters of the first order) and all social contexts work on each other. It is to search out what happens when a continuum of discourse both bespeaks itself and is bespoken. In *Doctor Zhivago*, Boris Pasternak suggested as well as anyone perhaps can what then happens. "At such moments," he says, "the correlation of the forces controlling the artist is, as it were, stood on its head. The ascendancy is no longer with the artist or the state of mind which he is trying to express, but with the language, his instrument of expression. Language, the dwelling place of beauty and meaning, itself begins to think and speak for man and turns wholly into music, not in the sense of outward, audible sounds but by virtue of the power and momentum of its inward flow. Then, like the current of a mighty river polishing stones and turning wheels by its very movement, the flow of speech creates in passing, by the force of its own laws, rhyme and rhythm and countless other forms and formations, still more important and until now undiscovered, unconsidered and unnamed."[27]

What happens in an act of language is not only a transfer of data from speaker to hearer, but a social transaction with reality whose ramifications escape over the horizon of the present and beyond the act of speech itself. The act changes the society in which it occurs. The society then adjusts to that change, becoming different from what it was before the act happened. This adjustment means that no subsequent act of language can ever touch the society in exactly the

86

same way as the previous act did. And it is in the constant adjustment to such change that a society increments its own awareness of its peculiar nature, that it shakes out and tests its own public and private norms, that it works out its sustained response to the phenomenon of its own existence in the real world. It is this ongoing adjustment which is the society's fundamental and most important business. It is where politics, morals, and all the arts are born. It is where all these, together with philosophy and religion, emerge in intimately related form, not yet separated out into competing and often contradictory "disciplines" which are by definition matters of the second order.

Similarly, one might set out to learn how baptism or eucharist or any of those other liturgical acts which, as we have seen, made up the whole round of a church's Sunday or festal worship reveal some crucial aspect of a Christian society's continuum of discourse in faith. Such acts affect this discourse and are affected by it, constitute it and give it shape. This would involve one in more than just seeking what the given liturgical act "means." It is to seek how liturgy "works" in and from its ecclesial context, and how all liturgical acts (matters of the first order) and all ecclesial contexts work on each other. It is to search for what happens when a continuum of faith-discourse bespeaks itself and is bespoken. At such moments, the correlation of forces controlling the worshipping assembly is, as it were, stood on its head. The ascendancy is no longer with the assembly or the state of corporate mind it may be trying to express, but with the liturgy, its instrument of expression. The liturgy, the dwelling place of present and remembered encounter with the living God, itself begins to think and speak for the assembly and turns wholly into music, not in the sense of outward, audible sounds, but by virtue of the power and momentum of its inward flow. Then, like the current of a mighty river polishing stones and turning wheels by its very movement, the flow of liturgical worship creates in passing, and by the force of its own laws, cadence and rhythm and countless other forms and formations, still more important and until now undiscovered, unconsidered, and unnamed.

What results from a liturgical act is not only "meaning," but an ecclesial transaction with reality, a transaction whose ramifications escape over the horizon of the present, beyond the act itself, to overflow even the confines of the local assembly into universality. The act both changes and outstrips the assembly in which it occurs. The assembly adjusts to that change, becoming different from what it was before the act happened. This adjustment means that subsequent acts of liturgy can never touch the assembly in exactly the same way as the previous act did. And it is in the constant adjustment to such change that an assembly increments its own awareness of its distinctive nature, that it shakes out and tests its own public and private norms of life and faith, that it works out its sustained response to the phenomenon of its own existence under God in the real world, a world whose Source is the same as that of the assembly itself. It is all this which is the ecclesial society's fundamental and most important business. It is where church order, mission, morals, ministry, and theology are born. It is where all these, together with cosmology and evangelism, emerge in intimately related form, not yet separated out into competing and often contradictory endeavors which are by definition matters of the second order.

So far three basic assertions have been made.

The first assertion distinguished two modes in theology. One was called secondary theology, about which we talk a lot. The other was called primary theology, about which we talk little if at all. Secondary theology is, moreover, not only something we talk about a lot but something which has become to a great extent the very way we think theologically. I find this highly developed, almost hypertrophied, linguistic and conceptual ocean about as difficult to emerge from as a fish would find it difficult to emerge from water. And as one does manage to emerge from it one finds oneself looking unlike anything else in the sea or on the shore. One emerges looking rather like an amphibian, a theological newt, fit to live only in the curricular swamps of something called "practical theology."

A second assertion concerned liturgy itself being not merely one *locus theologicus* among many but, in Schmemann's words, the very condition of doing theology, of understanding the Word of God. A liturgical act *is* a theological act of the most all-encompassing, integral, and foundational kind. It is both precipitator and result of that adjustment to the change wrought in the worshipping assembly by its regular encounter in faith with its divine Source. This adjustment to God-wrought change is no less critical and reflective an act of theology than any other of the secondary sort. Unlike these, however, it is *proletarian* in the sense that it is not done by academic elites; it is *communitarian* in the sense that it is not undertaken by the scholar alone in his study; and it is *quotidian* in the sense that it is not accomplished occasionally but regularly throughout the daily, weekly, and yearly round of the assembly's life of public liturgical worship. It is this constantly modulating, self-critical, and reflective adjustment to God-wrought change in the assembly's life of faith which constitutes the condition for doing all other forms of theology and of understanding the Word of God. It is not so much an isolated act as it is a state of continuing discourse within the worshipping fellowship, and the state is graced, self-critical, reflective, and altogether primary. It is the wellspring out of which the river of secondary theology arises and begins its flow by twists and turns to the sea. It is what liturgy enacts. It is what the secondary discipline known as liturgiology or liturgics studies; what gives the secondary discipline known as liturgical theology its material, purpose, and form. The closer these two secondary disciplines cleave to it the more helpful both are apt to be, the less they are apt to plunder the assembly's worship for polemical ends or warp the assembly and its worship into something neither can be and survive.

The immense gravitational pull exerted by secondary theology makes all this not easy to do. The results of our having all but given up trying to do it are all around us. The liturgical assembly is for the most part theologically disenfranchised, its constraining function largely ignored. The assembly's liturgy is often made up for it on the spot and reduced to aesthetic, educational, therapeutic, or ethical "messages" to the assembly, messages whose components can be separated, catalogued, and filed as diverse witnesses to this or that insight formulated by secondary theology. The assembly's own liturgical formulations about itself at worship—formulations such as traditions of piety expressed in rhetorical and ceremonial patterns of reverence, say, for the Mother of Jesus, or for the eucharistic presence, or for the dignity of the newly baptized—are reformed for it, discounted, or removed altogether as outdated or irrelevant. Secondary theology, even at its best, seems to approach the liturgical worship of Christians with a certain condescension and as not much more than a possible *locus theologicus* whose existence is to serve secondary theology and whose work must therefore be closely monitored.

90

A third assertion had to do with *orthodoxia* as a standard not primarily of correct belief but of "right worship." This root sense of the word firmly contextualizes it in the early Church's stress on faith not so much as an intellectual assent to doctrinal propositions, but as a way of living in the graced commonality of an actual assembly at worship before the living God. This stress is summed up in the patristic maxim *legem credendi lex statuat supplicandi*, a subtle formulation in which the predicate is all important. For the predicate *statuat* does not permit these two fundamental laws of belief and worship in Christian life to float apart or to be opposed to each other, as in the "tag" form *lex orandi, lex credendi*. The verb *statuat* articulates the standard of believing and the standard of worshipping within the faithful assembly. The agent of believing is no less communitarian than the agent of worship; the agent of the one is in fact the agent of the other. Since the agency of both is the same, the results of that agency must be seen as identical rather than as disparate and opposable. This is a cumbersome way of saying that a church assembled for worship commits, when it worships, an act of believing, an act of faith in the One who both summons the Church and enables its worship. The verb *statuat* subordinates the law of belief to the law of worship in just the same way, and for just the same reasons, as our reception of God's Word is subordinated to the presentation of that Word to us in the act of its being revealed and proclaimed to us. Belief is always consequent upon encounter with the Source of the grace of faith. Therefore Christians do not worship because they believe. They believe because the One in whose gift faith lies is regularly met in the act of communal worship—not because the assembly conjures up God, but because the intiative lies with the God who has promised to be there always. The *lex credendi* is thus subordinated to the *lex supplicandi* because both standards exist and function only within the worshipping assembly's own subordination of itself to its ever-present Judge, Savior, and unifying Spirit.

To reverse the maxim, subordinating the standard of worship to the standard of belief, makes a shambles of the dialectic of revelation. It was a Presence, not faith, which drew Moses to the burning bush, and what happened there was a revelation, not a seminar. It was a Presence, not faith, which drew the disciples to Jesus, and what happened then was not an educational program but his revelation to them of himself as the long-promised Anointed One, the redeeming because reconciling Messiah-Christos. Their lives, like that of Moses, were changed radically by that encounter with a Presence which upended all their ordinary expectations. Their descendants in faith have been adjusting to that change ever since, drawn into assembly by that same Presence, finding there always the troublesome upset of change in their lives of faith to which they must adjust still. Here is where their lives are regularly being constituted and reconstituted under grace. Which is why *lex supplicandi legem statuat credendi*.

There is no doubt that the law of belief does indeed shape and influence the law of worship. But the maxim does not say this, nor does it need to. It says only that the latter *constitutes* or *founds* the former. To reverse this is to cancel out the meaning of the maxim in its original formulation. The law of belief does *not* constitute the law of worship. Thus the creeds and the reasoning which produced them are not the forces which produced baptism. Baptism gave rise to the trinitarian creeds. So too the eucharist produced, but was not produced by, a scriptural text, the eucharistic prayer, or all the various scholarly theories concerning the eucharistic real presence. Influenced by, yes. Constituted or produced by, no. Creeds, theories, texts, and prayers all emerged from that dialectical process of change and adjustment to change triggered by the assembly's regular baptismal and eucharistic encounters with the living God in its own faithful life, a life embracing saints and sinners alike.

It is obvious that each of the three foregoing assertions deserves its own book. Making them on any less a scale runs the risk of foreshortening complex matters, and one should not do this except for good and sufficient reason. The reason for running the risk here is the hope that from the assertions' interplay an initial taxonomy of primary theology might emerge.

The taxonomy is operationally rhythmic. It begins with the act of liturgical worship. This act precipitates change in the liturgical assembly, change which is not so much immediately apparent, perhaps, as it is long-term, even eschatological, and inexorable. To such change the assembly adjusts through critical reflection upon its own stance in faith before the God who gifts the assembly with its own existence and with a created world in which to stand and minister before him. The faithful assembly brings all this with it to its next act of worship, an act which then precipitates further change and adjustment, recapitulating what went before. Although this is only a schema, what is being schematized is a regular, ongoing process of experience, memory, reflection, and reappropriation carried out by real people in always changing circumstances which affect the process and are affected by it. This is how the assembly constructs its own story, its history, and in the construction constantly rediscovers and constitutes itself under grace for the life of the world.

The taxonomy possesses certain definite qualities. As we have suggested, it is *proletarian* rather than elitist, *communitarian* rather than individualistic or idiosyncratic, *quotidian* rather than random or

infrequent. There is in addition a certain *violence*
involved in it. It follows a law of change even unto
death rather than the stately laws of organic evolution,
much less the totalitarian imperatives of scientific
determinism. The worshipping assembly is neither a
machine nor a species of plant. It is a human society
suffused with the unpredictable presence of One who
is not content with remaining a first principle, a ground
of being, or a transcendent way, but who had the
effrontery to take flesh and pitch his tent beside ours.
And whom we crucified. This endows the assembly
with a certain *wariness* because it teaches the assembly
that, as someone has said, the Tree of Life is filled with
a million mouths.

The taxonomy expresses itself in monuments of
ceremony and art which remain largely anonymous in
their authorship, obscure in their intention, and
ambiguous in their meaning. These characteristics
invest the taxonomy's expressive monuments with that
curious power which we moderns perhaps sense most
when we confront "primitive" artifacts such as tribal
masks, pre-Columbian statues, or aboriginal totems in
museums. These also are largely anonymous, obscure,
and ambiguous. When we categorize these things as
"primitive," we should be aware that what we really
mean is that their manifest sophistication runs along
tracks to which we have no access, that we have no
intelligibility structures sufficiently developed to allow
us to housebreak them, so to speak, within our own
shrunken range of cultural discourse. This is why they
frighten the altar guild. That it never crosses our minds
that a liturgy or an icon should cause us to shiver only
shows how we have allowed ourselves to tame the Lion
of Judah and put him into a suburban zoo to entertain
children.

The taxonomy, finally, has an effect. It is a life of
orthodoxia which has been called one, holy, catholic,

and apostolic. These adjectives, worn slick with use, mean that a life of right worship is a life of communion in all God's holy things and among his holy persons. That it is open unalterably to all people everywhere without let or hindrance. That its memory is not short but long, stretching back through all those whom Jesus Christ sent first, encompassing all those he has sent since, and mindful of all those whom he will send in the future. The only way in which such a life can be sustained in all its openness, totality, sacredness, and sent purpose is by the constancy of its standing in the presence of its Source, of its suffering whatever change that Source chooses to work within it, and of its painful coming to terms with that change. This last is where the assembly's faith is translated into existential fidelity to its Source by graced acts on its own part which are reflective, self-critical, and wholly theological.

Thus is the faith kept as something always alive in the present. Thus is memory mediated ever new as tradition. Thus is conversion made a sustained quality in the assembly itself. Thus is divine purpose served in the real world of whatever epoch. Thus is the Gift always given and received. Thus do structures arise. Hence theology of the second order flows.

Perhaps now a more detailed taxonomy of the liturgy may itself be discovered.

Chapter Six

Liturgy of God or about God

Since liturgy occupies so central a place in the foregoing construct of a life of *orthodoxia*, liturgy now needs its own taxonomy which might support the claim made for it. The claim is that a liturgical act is the act of primary theology par excellence, the act from which other acts of secondary theology take their rise within that life of right worship we call the worshipping assembly, the community of faith, the Church. In this chapter I will suggest an analogy between liturgy and holy scripture. In the following chapter I will discuss liturgy's canonical structure. In the final chapter I will try to outline liturgy's fundamental operation.

In a recent small book I compared liturgy and language in order to mount an essay on the grammar and syntax of liturgical style in practice.[28] As language exists first of all not to be written or analyzed but to be spoken, so also a liturgy exists first of all not to be read or studied but to be done. If they are anything, liturgy and language are media of communication, and to communicate is to do something, to act. This act involves one in social relations, which are never without pattern, rules, conditions, and sanctions. This is so because of the social nature of communication itself. Language and society are, it seems, coterminous in origin and very nearly convertible as terms. It is no more possible to conceive of a society without some form of communicative language than it is to conceive of a language whose motive and effects are asocial.

Such thoughts suggest that an aliturgical Christian church is as much a contradiction in terms as a human society without language. By this I mean something harder and more definite than the general assertion that Christians worship. I mean that *ecclesia* and *leitourgia* are coterminous in origin and very nearly convertible as terms. The community in which my faith is worked out is Christian because the cult it practices is Christian throughout. My cultural community is fundamentally Anglo-Saxon because the language it speaks is English, the Anglo-Saxon tongue. Another's cultural community may be fundamentally Hispanic or Germanic because it speaks Spanish or German. The patterns by which we communicate lock us into social traditions which in turn endow us with identity and perspective. Those patterns by which we communicate are, moreover, constantly constituting and reinforcing social traditions day to day; they are not optional or accidental to those social traditions but constitutive of them. When language lapses, the community it constitutes disperses. In this sense a human community does not merely use a language; it *is* the language it speaks. Similarly, a Christian church does not merely use a liturgy; it *is* the liturgy by which it worships.

In this connection it is often useful to remember that Jesus the Christ did not bid farewell to his friends at an ordinary meal to which some worship elements had been added *ad libitum* on the spur of the moment or as an afterthought. The burden of New Testament evidence points to his having chosen their community's traditional Passover seder (and seder means order of service) to give concrete and perennial form to the new relationship he had come to establish between God and our race—a relationship not of deity to devotees, nor of sovereign to subjects, nor of general to troops, but a relationship between friends at dinner.[29] The Church came into visible, overt, and accessible existence in a formal liturgical event carried out according to Jewish rubrics around a table which orthodox Christians have kept in their midst ever since.

Christians do not succumb to the grace of faith first and then sort out what their options for worship might be. Augustine worshipped with the faithful for years before he finally succumbed to the grace of faith, as he tells us, on the occasion of hearing a child's voice singing in the distance "Take and read, take and read." What he read was the Bible which he had already heard read out in worship over and over again since he himself was a child, and more lately heard preached in public worship by the great Ambrose of Milan. Throughout Augustine's own life as a rather wandering catechumen for thirty years, he had been deeply enfolded by the church's *lex supplicandi*. As he himself tells, the sound of Christians singing and the thunder of their Amens rolling through the basilicas in which they worshipped moved him farther toward faith than did his own sharp-edged arguments against the Manichees. In fact, the church's *lex supplicandi* was during this whole time constituting a *lex credendi* in Augustine's life which became finally irresistible. So far from being separable, the two laws were but distinct and correlative facets of one and the same grace: faith originating in God and communicated incarnationally through human means which were themselves suffused with faith.

The result was that Augustine found himself being baptized and communicated at Ambrose's hands in the midst of those whose singing and Amens had helped bring him home. Years later, he spoke to these nameless people on the anniversary of his having become their bishop. "When it dismays me that I am here for you," he said, "it consoles me that I am with you. For you I am a bishop, but with you I am a Christian. The first is an office accepted, the second a grace received; the one is a danger, the other a safety. We are tossed, it is true, as in a high sea by the storms of our toil. But as we recall whose blood it was that bought us, we come through the calm of that thought safely into harbor. And as we labor at this task of ours, our response is the benefit we all share. If, then, I am gladder by far to be redeemed with you than I am to be placed over you, I shall be more completely your servant as the Lord commanded for fear of being ungrateful for the price that was paid to save me that I might be yours."[30]

Having said that Christians do not worship because they believe, I must also say that Christians do not believe because they worship, at least in the sense that liturgy is a machine which can be counted on to produce a product called faith on any and all occasions. This would be a sort of liturgical Pelagianism. Augustine had for years thought long and hard about pressing philosophical issues, but it was not until the church's *lex supplicandi* threw flashes of light, coherence, and congruence into the total life of Augustine the thinker that Augustine the human being was able to see that he had been in the presence of God all along, walking with him and even sitting at his table. The Church's discipline of worship did not produce Augustine's faith, but it does seem to have prodded its emergence, given it its foundation in the real order of the time, and shaped it to the point that it became recognizable to Augustine himself and accessible to others. And it seems that Monica, his mother, was able to see all this happening more clearly than Augustine himself, she being a practitioner of the *lex supplicandi* if there ever was one.

The worship and belief of Christians converge, meet, entwine, and meld in their liturgical act. This act is not reducible to conceptual propositions, for what is the creed without baptism? This act, so viewed, is not reducible to prayer, for many important elements native to the act itself are demonstrably not prayers. This act, so viewed, is not even reducible to worship, for many of its elements are not worship acts in themselves but elements which can be said to be at best preparatory for worship in public, as distinct from worship in the privacy of one's own closet. A liturgical act is not simply a creed, a prayer, or worship without qualification. A liturgical act which is the convergence, meeting, entwining, and melding of Christian worship and belief—in other words an enactment of that *lex supplicandi* which forms and constitutes but does not "produce" the *lex credendi*—is a fourth thing. It is *rite*.

Rite involves creeds and prayers and worship, but it is not any one of these things, nor all of these things together, and it orchestrates more than these things. Rite can be called a whole style of Christian living found in the myriad particularities of worship, of laws called "canonical," of ascetical and monastic structures, of evangelical and catechetical endeavors, and in particular ways of doing secondary theological reflection. A liturgical act concretizes all these and in doing so makes them accessible to the community assembled in a given time and place before the living God for the life of the world. Rite in this Christian sense is generated and sustained in this regular meeting of faithful people in whose presence and through whose deeds the vertiginous Source of the cosmos itself is pleased to settle down freely and abide as among friends. A liturgy of Christians is thus nothing less than the way a redeemed world is, so to speak, done. The liturgical act of rite and the assembly which does it are coterminous, one thing: the incorporation under grace of Christ dying and rising still, restoring the communion all things and persons have been gifted with in Spirit and in truth. A liturgy is even more than an act of faith, prayer, or worship. It is an act of rite.

This understanding of rite is hardly common today. One reason for this may be that it is so hard to put into words in a culture for which the term rite suggests ritual, something which means thoughtless repetition of irrelevant because mindless reactionism. It is what Archie Bunkers do best. Even among Christians who profess to take worship seriously, ritual is often regarded as *adiaphora*, unessential, and to be treated warily if at all. Ritual, and by implication rite, seem to be the antithesis of enlightenment and freedom.

What has happened to our grasp of rite may be similar to what happens to the grasp of language on the part of those who know nothing more about it than how to process words on a machine. Language disintegrates among them rather as rite has done among us. We can see only its myriad liturgical parts—calendars, seasons, prayers, rubrics, gestures, ministries, music, artifacts, appurtenances, vestments, schedules, tastes, bread recipes, banners, fads, epicleses, books; how and where to receive communion and from whom, choosing anthems, where to reserve the sacrament, deacons and what to do with them, when to have confirmation; public address systems, dance teams, slide projectors, missalettes, movie cameras, arts and crafts. Our ability to grasp the whole is inhibited by many of these things having their own special interest groups intent upon getting their own particular issue advanced to special status. Rite becomes a littered battleground upon which there are no victors; only the blinded and bemused picking over rubble where villages of coherence once stood.

Those who are sincerely concerned with the Gospel of Jesus Christ may be forgiven for keeping their distance from all this. They have always done so, and this may be one reason for the general absence of commentary on liturgical mutation at those very points in history where we know that the liturgy was undergoing significant evolution within a context of cultural shift. Those of us today who think of ourselves as standing in the sanctuary rather than in the nave of the Church (and by no means are all of us ordained clerics) must not forget that what exercises us about the liturgy rarely exercises everyone else, that everyone else is in the vast majority and always has been, and that the great unwritten tradition of common sense seems to be on their side. Rite is sustained by rote and obedience far more than by restless creativity, and obedience is a subordinate part of the larger virtue of justice while creativity is not. In our day it seems to require more courage to obey a rubric or law than to break it. Creativity of the Spontaneous Me variety condemns rite and symbol to lingering deaths by trivialization, bemusing those who would communicate by rite and symbol to a point where they finally wander away in search of something which appears to be more stable and power-laden.

The trivialization of rite and the symbols it uses adds greatly to the already serious difficulties which otherwise inhibit a liturgical act being taken seriously by secondary theologians. It is as though the Hebrew and Christian scriptures had been broken up into a random collection of anecdotes whose purpose is low edification for adults and entertainment for children in Sunday schools. Anything going beyond this would then be regarded as an unwarranted imposition, an act of oppression committed by fanatical ecclesiastics opposed to edification and necessary childish fun, a conspiracy against the virtue of informal sharing, a

102

refusal to allow people to grow and learn, an inhuman tyranny run by those who take seriously those things in which no one else is interested, which no one else needs. It is the argument from relevance, and it ends by subordinating the Passover of Christ to an Easter egg hunt, by cashing in the deposit of faith sustained over centuries in the tactful rhetoric of ordinary believers to buy into an emotional fast-food franchise renamed The Church.

To go on in this vein is a temptation which must be resisted lest it overpower the analogy I wish to mount. It is an analogy between liturgy as rite on one hand and scripture on the other. By it I hope to suggest some reasons why secondary theology ought to take rite more seriously than is usually the case.

We are accustomed to taking scripture much more seriously than rite. One reason for this is the thoroughly bad press liturgical rite received during the Renaissance and Reformation, a bad press which was not wholly undeserved. Western liturgy at the end of the Middle Ages was seriously hypertrophied, which means that there was simply more of it around than any but ecclesiastical experts could bear. With only a few exceptions, even these knew relatively little about the liturgy itself; thus they often overcompensated in their attacks on it or defense of it. The liturgy was inexorably brought into disrepute by both sides in the debate between new devotion and learning and the old, between Reformers and Catholics.

But an even more important development than liturgical hypertrophy was Europe's unavoidable slide into textual absorption, something stimulated by the invention of printing. Northern Europeans became literary humanists rather as southern Europeans had become aesthetic humanists, and proponents of the Reformation were largely men of the north who fell as easily into textual obsession with the Bible as they did into mistrust of urbane aesthetes from south of the Alps. The technology of printing helped to blow apart a moribund medieval world, unleashing forces which the modern world copes with uneasily still. And while it would be too much to say that printing reduced God's Word into words, since writing itself was responsible for that, it would be true to say that printing turned God's Words into a text which all people, literate or not, could now see as lines of type marching across a page. God's Word could now for the first time be visualized by all, not in the multivalency of a "presence" in corporate act or icon,[31] but linearly in horizontal lines which could be edited, reset, revised, fragmented, and studied by all—something which few could have done before. A Presence which had formerly been experienced by most as a kind of enfolding embrace had now modulated into an abecedarian printout to which only the skill of literacy could give complete access. God could now be approached not only through burning bushes, sacralized spaces, and holy symbols and events, but through texts so cheaply reproduced as to be available to all. Rite and its symbols could be displaced or got round altogether, and so could the whole of the living tradition which provided the gravitational field holding them together in an intelligible union. Rite became less a means than an obstacle for the new textual piety. And once rite receded, so did the need for that kind of assembly whose common burden was the enactment of rite rather than attendance upon didactic exposition of set texts. The truth lies now exclusively in the text; no longer on the walls, or in the windows, or in the liturgical activity of those who occupy the churches.[32] Protestant iconoclasm was thus not, nor could it have been, selective or corrective. It was programmatic and across the board. It did not modify an old equation but wrote a new one.

Liturgical hypertrophy and the invention of printing by movable type were not, of course, the only factors involved in the reform movements of Catholics and Protestants during the sixteenth century and after. But when one tries to account for the fate of rite and symbol in Reformation and Counter-Reformation churches, the combined effects of liturgical hypertrophy and printing technology cannot be ignored safely. The two factors meshed. The technology of printing made it possible to put the texts of pruned liturgies into the hands of worshippers very quickly indeed for the first time ever and at rapidly decreasing cost. This rendered the extensive, complex, and expensive libraries of liturgical books which were needed for full celebration of the old liturgy obsolete in one stroke, as Archbishop Cranmer noted in the preface of the new English Book of Common Prayer of 1549. It also greatly speeded up liturgical change by giving this previously labyrinthine and long-term process over to committees of experts whose work was predominantly textual and theological rather than ritual and symbolic. This in turn made the liturgy of Christians much easier to control by positive ecclesiastical law administered through centralized bureaucratic offices of church government, something which was, as we have noted, largely unknown until then.

The liturgy was thus constricted to a set of texts which could not only be put cheaply into the hands of each member of the assembly, but which could be altered quickly and controlled effectively even down to the details of layout and typography by groups of experts whose competencies were often tangential to the rite itself. Under such conditions, the liturgical action tended to shrink from being a complex diversity of intermeshing ministries and roles working together toward common ritual and symbolic purpose,[33] to concern itself more with the individual reaction of the worshipper to a text held in the hand and followed with the eye. Sermons, exhortations, and biblical readings could be followed with the eye as they were being read aloud by the minister. The liturgy began to shift from rite as an enacted style of common life carried on in rich symbolic ambiguity to the simultaneous reading and recitation of printed texts which were increasingly didactic in nature. Being subject to official change (Cranmer significantly reformed the Book of Common Prayer of 1549 again in 1552), an increasingly textual liturgy was liable to be relativized as theological positions and their political effects changed. This situation, which was by no means unique to England in the sixteenth century, dismayed many, exhilarated some, and loosened the social bonds which rite previously had helped to maintain among believers of diverse sorts from southern Italy to northern Scotland.

It is not easy for us who live on this side of the invention of printing to sense how very novel this sort of liturgy was to one who had never seen liturgical texts during worship but had only heard them, to one who therefore never felt compelled to sit still in ranks of immovable pews resembling lines of type marching across a page and to follow what was being said aloud by watching a text or reading a score. When we encounter such people today, as in parts of Italy, Greece, the Middle East, Russia, and elsewhere, their liturgical worship strikes us as helter-skelter and somehow impious. They move around in churches largely empty of pews doing a variety of dubious things, coming and going, apparently taking the service so lightly (except at certain moments) that they seem unconcerned. Augustine said that they talked during his sermons. John Chrysostom mentions that they cheered, wept, pounded their breasts audibly, and otherwise carried on during his. *Ordo Romanus I* implies that they were apt to steal even the gospel book during papal masses in the seventh century. They have been known to become rowdy when presbyters or deacons omitted something, to kidnap celebrants for one reason or another, and Augustine mentions that they stank so badly in the heat of a North African August that he had to leave the building. They met liturgically in tenements (*tituli*), forums, piazzi, welfare centers (*diaconiae*), streets, shrines, cemeteries, and cathedrals. Their worship spilled over into entire cities and their suburbs to become a movable feast which took most of the day. As we have noted, it was less a single service like ours than it was a whole series of interlocking services which began at dawn and ended only with sundown, when all civil business ceased. Everyone attended some of it. Only the remarkably pious attended it all.

This is what Christian rite had evolved into by the sixth century. It was episcopal rather than parochial in our modern sense and thoroughly urban. Its ministers each had their own appropriate liturgical book; everyone else knew their own parts by heart. This was the sort of liturgy which generated the main families of liturgical rites as we know them: the Roman, Byzantine, Antiochene, Alexandrian, Edessan (East Syrian), Palestinian (Jerusalem), and their derivatives. The barbarian peoples which settled Europe and Russia from the fifth through the eighth centuries were influenced by them and strove to imitate them as the Middle Ages wore on, scaling them down into their own nonurban modes of life and adding to them from their own burgeoning repertoire of local usage and rich if sometimes startling folk piety. This was the process which was largely responsible for that hypertrophy mentioned earlier as a significant liturgical problem by the time of the Renaissance in the West. It was something which the Roman Church ignored at times, frowned on at others, but could do little about prior to the Council of Trent, since liturgical regulation before that time was carried on not by general legislation but by traditional, yet far from slavish, deference to the prestige of Roman usage as locally interpreted—in such centers as Salisbury (Sarum), Hereford, Bangor, York, and Lincoln in England; in Lyons, Seville, Paris, Milan, Trondheim, Metz, Mainz, and elsewhere on the continent. There were even a variety of Roman usages in the city of Rome itself. One of these, the rite of the papal court, was spread by itinerant Franciscans from the thirteenth century throughout Europe and would become the basis for reform during and after the Council of Trent.[34] The political, technological, cultural, and religious upheavals of the late fifteenth and sixteenth centuries swept much of this away, ushering in the situation under which we labor even now.

All this may indicate, even in a schematic manner, that there was rather more afoot in the sixteenth century than some disagreements over justification, the real presence of Christ in the eucharist, and papal primacy. A sense of rite and symbol in the West was breaking down and under siege. And since it now appears that those who sought to repair the breakdown were its products rather than its masters, they may be said with greater accuracy to have substituted something in its place that was new and, to them, more relevant to the times. It was a new system of worship which would increasingly do without rite, one in which printed texts would increasingly bear the burden formerly borne by richly ambiguous corporate actions done with water, oil, food, and the touch of human hands. *Orthodoxia* as a life of right worship modulated into a literate effort at remaining doctrinally correct. Worship provided the prime occasion during the week at which this literate effort could be exercised by giving austere attention to biblical texts under the tutelage of a learned ministry. The Bible became the syllabus by which ordained educators could instruct their unordained (and thus by implication unlearned) charges about doctrinal orthodoxy within a doxological setting whose other words and ceremonies were expendable. Liturgy had begun to become "worship," and worship to become scripture's stepchild rather than its home. And the primary theological act which the liturgical act had once been now began to be controlled increasingly by practitioners of secondary theology whose concerns lay with correct doctrine in a highly polemical climate.

The taxonomy of primary theology which has been advanced in the previous chapter was altered in some parts and reversed in others as secondary theology took over. Its rhythm slowly ceased to operate. It became elitist, individualistic, even idiosyncratic; occasional according to educational or polemical needs (as in services to raise people's consciousness concerning issues sanctioned by largely academic elites); suffused with the placid respectability of academe and the need for comfort of the middle class. It was expressed increasingly in signed monuments such as hymns and prayers by identified composers in which symbolic ambiguity was forced to recede before conceptual precision. And the power of communal activity built up and magnified in a shared tradition over generations mutated into the power of individual concepts enunciated by major scholars, composers, theological schools of thought, and authoritative ecclesiastical bureaucracies such as Sacred Congregations and societies for the promotion of Christian this or that.

Primary theology was being reduced inexorably to secondary place and secondary theology was beginning to set the agenda for that educational event which liturgical worship was becoming. The *orthodoxia* of rite was dissolving and being reassembled as an *orthopistis* or *orthodidascalia* of concepts and methods controlled by learned ministers, professors, and ecclesiastical boards to be purveyed through a system of parochial "outlets" to those who, through no fault of their own, lacked certification as experts. These people constituted the proletariat of the merely baptized who were expected to bring their study texts—their Bibles, prayerbooks, and layfolk's missals—with them and to sit, schoolroom fashion, in rows of linotypical pews to be instructed by the knowing in the unknown.

In such an atmosphere, it is not surprising that other dimensions of rite began to fall away. The year with its liturgical seasons, feasts, and fasts was gradually replaced with secular or educational surrogates. Vestments faded or became ecclesiastical costumery, processions ceased or withdrew to the interiors of churches, affective devotion went out of style. Eucharistic dining became little more than eating in memory of an absent Friend. Marriage sank into a stale formality as the family bond loosened and children came to be regarded either as pets or as a serious nuisance. People finally stopped coming to church for education and started going to graduate school. Popular culture suppressed social sanctions as personally oppressive and then succumbed to stress and anxiety without them. Ministerial preparation shrank into a sixteenth-century invention, the seminary, where alone true Christians were now to be found. Parishes became centers for education, social service, or cultural uplift where worship had to be commended as speaking to fluctuating human needs. *Sola scriptura* churches realized that they often had more Bach than Bible, and that the latter had migrated into Fundamentalism or passed back, oddly, into the possession of the old churches which had never taken *sola scriptura* seriously to begin with. This last rather

110

ironic development perhaps signals that the printed text, which may have made the notion of *sola scriptura* possible in the first place, is losing its grip on modern minds as technology forsakes print for electronic systems whose "printouts" are convertible into images. An image, it is said, is worth a thousand words. This may be one reason why, at latest count, some 20 percent of Americans in this television age are reputed to be functionally illiterate.

Breaking down the western dichotomy between precise text and ambiguous image may make it possible to discuss scripture and liturgy as correlative aspects of rite and as yoked generators of *orthodoxia* once again. Such a discussion would have to begin by shedding our fixation with scripture as a text from which Christian liturgy somehow results as effect from cause. Short of this, it will not be possible to grasp the fact that before any books of the Christian Bible had been produced, Christian liturgy had already been not only conceived within the womb of Judaism but had also been born and had grown into a vigorous youth. It had already formed for itself liturgical hymns, prayers, structures, and procedure (e.g., for catechesis, baptism, and eucharist) to which evangelists, apostolic writers, and others could refer in the scriptural writings. Liturgy and scripture were compenetrating endeavors in earliest Christianity no less than they had always been in Judaism. The agent of each was the believing community within which patriarchs, prophets, kings, virgins, evangelists, wives, mothers, apostles, and all others lived, moved, worshipped and worked out their existence. Scripture and liturgy were each part and parcel of what has here been called rite, that is, the whole style of life found in the myriad particularities of worship, law, ascetical and monastic structures, evangelical and catechetical endeavors, and in particular ways of theological reflection. Scripture reflects all this. Liturgy concretizes all these as well as scripture too. In doing so, liturgy makes them all regularly accessible to those who assemble within such a particular style of life, be it at Jerusalem, Ephesus, Corinth, Rome, Constantinople, New York, London, or Hong Kong.

Having shed our constricting fixation with scripture as nothing but a text, the discussion of it and liturgy will be in a better position to recover the appreciation of earlier centuries that God's most complete self-revelation was neither in words nor in print but amid a people and in the flesh. The Word became flesh and dwelt in our midst, where we saw more of Its glory and Its pathos than we perhaps cared to see. Not only did we hear him speak, we saw him act, and in acting he spoke more forcefully than words could. The One who was the ultimate source of Judaic rite, the very content of Judaic symbol, poured himself out to take his place in solidarity with others as a member of that rite, as a user and sustainer and renovator of its symbols. Because of who he was, he could say to his colleagues when he had read to them from Isaiah in the synagogue on a Sabbath, "Today in your hearing is this text fulfilled." All our words about God had become a present and living Word who walked our roads, entered our house, and sat at our table.

The link between scripture and liturgy is found in the radical incarnationalism expressed in Chalcedonian language by the Second Vatican Council's statement *Dei Verbum* 13: "For the words of God, expressed in human language, have been made like human discourse, just as of old the Word of the eternal Father, when he took to Himself the weak flesh of humanity, became like other men."[35] Raymond Brown interprets this to mean that God does not merely *use* a human medium such as a human nature, a writing, or (I add) a liturgical event to disclose himself as it were from afar.

Rather, God welds himself into the human medium while never becoming subordinate to it.[36] *Dei Verbum,* moreover, places deeds alongside words in describing biblical revelation, both of them fully human but "of God." The meaning of both deeds and words is God's meaning, but the deeds and words which manifest the divine meaning are also fully human and thus fully subject to all the limitations that go with being human. "There is a *kenōsis,*" Brown says, "involved in God's committing His message to human words."[37]

I add that there must also be a corresponding *kenōsis* in committing oneself to a liturgical deed which has God so welded to itself that it too manifests consistently the reality of God's own kenotic union with our race—in the loving word of the Law within Israel, in the living Word of the incarnate Jesus in the world, in the judging Word of the risen Christ within the Church. Like the biblical word, like the incarnate Word, like the judging risen Word, the liturgy of the Church of Christ is more of God than about God. Biblical word, incarnate Word, risen Word, and liturgy of the Word are all the more fully human because they are fully of God. The liturgy of the table is called divine by many Eastern Churches for a good reason.

That the liturgy, like the Bible, the incarnation, and the Church, is more of God than about God (as are the interpretations of councils and theologians) is a notion which may rest uneasily on modern minds. The notion definitely puts liturgy within the *taxis* or category of realities which are fundamental and irreducibly primary in Christian life. It implies that liturgy is all that worship is, but more; that while liturgy (like the Bible and the incarnation) is for us rather than we are for the liturgy (or the Bible or the incarnation), neither liturgy nor Bible nor incarnation are for us to be done with as we wish. They, like the Sabbath, are our summons home to a community of Three Persons who remain present to, for, and with us at every step along the way.

Nor are Bible and incarnation any less subject in their own ways to human limitations than is the liturgy. The Bible may be inspired and inerrant, but it is not without the quirks and special viewpoints of its many human authors. The incarnate Word may have been impeccable, but he was not impassible. The liturgy of the Church of Christ may be divine, but its transactions are cast necessarily in the particularities of various human epochs and cultures, particularities which modulate over the years. Why the liturgy's own proper human limitations should be singled out as reasons why it alone must be merely about God rather than of God is a question not answered readily. It may be that certain critics find in the liturgy certain things, such as a strong tradition of deepest veneration for the Mother of Jesus, with which they disagree. But others have found difficulties no less severe with the Bible, and the incarnate Word himself never managed to elicit complete agreement with his teachings among his own contemporaries, even among his own disciples.

My own opinion concerning why the liturgy has been reduced to being merely about God rather than of God has already been advanced. It was due, namely, to a particular human limitation known as liturgical hypertrophy during the later medieval period together with the collapse of the medieval world and the revolution in communications caused by the technology of printing. These factors working in concert diminished the West's sense of rite and its grasp on its symbolic vocabulary, something which in turn shifted the nature of religious perception. Of this diminished sense of rite the hypertrophied liturgy in the West was both a cause and an effect which became so evident that it attracted more than ordinary attention from those who sought either to restore or to alter the old order. The polemical climate which ensued in the sixteenth century and after was one which had little patience with the very way in which liturgy carries on its transactions with the realities of faith in the real world among ordinary believers. Liturgy is not a very effective polemical tool unless one changes it into what I have called an exercise in doxological education. Catholics have called the liturgy the main organ of the Church's "ordinary magisterium," that is, the usual and regular way in which the entire assembly of believers communicates within itself the truths of its faith and life in Christ both locally and universally. As such, Christians in the act of liturgical worship, standing in the divine presence under grace, authentically interpret the Word of God, whether written or incarnate or handed on in the tradition of other such assemblies doing the same thing. This regular interpretative function is a primary theological endeavor which does not place the liturgy apart from or above God's Word. Rather, the liturgical act of rite coordinates the various modalities by which that saving Word is manifested as written, incarnate, and risen within the context of a living community of believers in that Word, making that Word accessible to them on a regular basis as in no other way. The liturgical act serves the Word intimately because it is of God rather than merely about God.

But the liturgy clearly does not do this as does the "extraordinary magisterium," which acts in special and infrequent ways such as in papal, episcopal, and conciliar pronouncements on doctrine and discipline, nor as do individual theologians. The liturgy does not analyze, explain, propound propositions, or polemicize. It does not attempt to educate in a didactic manner or to be commended in a public relations manner. It supports, forms, and nurtures by engaging people in communal acts within which the whole of rite as I have described it comes into motion. The liturgy cracks open radical values, invites without coercing people into them, and celebrates their living presence deep within these same values. Therefore what the liturgy does lies closer to the general intent of God's Word written, incarnate, and risen in his Church than do even the best efforts of Popes, councils, polemicists, theologians, or educators. Thus the liturgy does not merely talk about God, but manifests the assembly's graced union with Father, through Son, in Spirit. It is, in this sense and in solidarity with holy scripture, the incarnation, and the Church, more of God than about God.

When the liturgy moves or is moved from being of God to being about God, that is, when it shifts toward being some form of education done in a doxological context for ideological ends, then significant mutations begin to occur. Concepts become more precise, the assembly more passive, ministries more learned, sermons more erudite, and pews fixed. Texts proliferate, the sonic arts of liturgical oratory and the kinetic arts of ceremony fade, and people find themselves in church to receive a message rather than to do, somehow, the World according to divine pleasure. The liturgical anchor of rite begins to drag and all those other facets of rite— law, ascetical and monastic structures, evangelical and catechetical endeavors—begin to collapse or disappear. Even particular ways or idioms of theological reflection desert the pulpit to become no longer a pastoral but an academic effort. Rite's surrogate becomes civil religion filtered somewhat, softened somewhat, by a generally benign middle-class liberalism in danger of becoming defensive, inbred, and infertile because it is no longer brought into vigorous confrontation with the Gospel but has become the only way in which the Gospel is to be understood. The Church becomes a clergy support group. The center no longer holds. Christianity becomes one telegram of consolation among others rather than a sustained experience of the presence of the living God, an experience which is itself the corporate message a liberated People proclaim in a world snared in thickets of its own making.

This chapter began with a taxonomy of liturgy which might undergird the liturgy's being construed as the primary theological act of a life of one, holy, catholic, and apostolic right worship or *orthodoxia*. The taxonomic discussion began by suggesting that language and liturgy, both of which are systems of communication, are analogues, whatever the other differences might be which set them apart. As language, that is, the act of speech, anchors even larger dimensions of human intercourse in society and culture, so also liturgy anchors even larger dimensions of human intercourse in faith, larger dimensions I have referred to collectively as rite—that whole style of Christian living in a particular idiom of ecclesial engagement, be it Coptic or Mozarabic, Byzantine or Roman, Milanese or Armenian, and so forth.

I tried to be candid about the difficulties we moderns have when we try to attain so holistic a notion of liturgy and rite. Our minds, it seems, were significantly altered on such matters by various factors which built up a critical mass during and after the Renaissance of the fifteenth and sixteenth centuries in the West. What emerged from this period of immense stress was a rather novel form of endeavor known as "worship" rather than "liturgy" in its previously understood sense. The result was that western Christianity as a whole, and the various Protestant churches in particular, embarked upon a hitherto unknown way of dealing with the Word of God in its written, incarnate, and ecclesial manifestations. This way was, due to the nature of the new "worship," increasingly shorn of the witness of rite as I have tried to describe it. The place vacated by rite was gradually taken over by the witness of texts of various sorts, texts which were designed, approved, and authentically interpreted no longer by the sustained liturgical *gestes* of the faithful assembly itself but by the growing body of precise, didactic, and normative theological formulations emanating from academic, bureaucratic, and other ecclesiastical bodies and enforced by law. Secondary theological influence increased greatly, primary theology receded. The *orthodoxia* of rite, anchored in the assembly's liturgical act, dissolved to be reassembled as an orthodoxy of concepts, propositions, and approved insights.[38]

The situation this produced not only allowed but forced elements which had formerly coexisted modestly as complementary parts of a much greater whole to drift apart, to become opposed, or even to die out. Thus word and sacrament could become, for the first time ever, antithetical, an antithesis which produced churches in which the one could be played off against the other, exploited independently, and finally result in one church being as uneasy with Word as another is with sacrament. Checks and balances were lost, idiosyncrasies multiplied, worship services finally were made up on the spot and for one time only. Secondary theology, constantly under pressure to be a surrogate for rite, discovered itself to be prone to faddish conceptual orthodoxies in danger of being steadily denatured.

Where liturgy waned into a form of doxological education conducted by secondary theologians who possessed academic degrees rather than ritual-sacramental power, the written Word of God degenerated into a disputed text first among polemicists, then among exegetes, and more lately into a quasi-scientific tract by which Fundamentalists try to confound Darwin in order to protect themselves in a pluralistic society. Rite and its liturgical enactment ceased to be scripture's home and became its stepchild first, then its third cousin, and finally an unrecognized stranger.

I suggested that the link between scripture and liturgy can probably never be recovered and sustained unless we shed our fixation on scripture as a printed text. I do not mean something negative or anti-intellectual by this. Scripture-as-text has always had high importance for ascetics and scholars, and it always will. But the high-water mark of God's self-revelation nonetheless came not in the form of spoken or written or printed words. It came in the flesh of one called the Word, who made of those believing in him his own body corporate, a People of the Word. Those who are baptized and anointed in him, who are constantly nourished at his table, are the corporate presence by faith and grace of God's Word incarnate still in the world. There will never be any greater self-disclosure on God's part than this. In the incarnation of his Son the living God has been pleased to weld us into himself and fill us with his Spirit, which is a consolation. But that in doing so he never becomes subordinate to us is fearsome.

There is nothing unusual about a deity being fearsome. Deities are well known for this quality. Nor is there anything unusual about a deity consoling its devotees. But there does seem to be something unusual about the way in which the God of Jesus Christ is fearsome with such tenderness, consoling with such towering justice. The perfect icon of this is painted by the Christian Bible three times: in the accounts of Jesus' birth, his transfiguration, and his death and resurrection. The perfect enactment of this is the liturgy of Christians. For when they come to their liturgy, Christians approach not just a text, a proposition, a doctrine, an option, or a chance to grab the brass ring of grace or passing moral uplift. In their liturgy, Christians disport themselves warily with One for whom their universe is but the snap of a finger. They have the impertinence to play with the One who did not hesitate to yield up his only Son into our bloodstained hands. This is the One at whose table we sit by grace and pardon.

As Christians have traditionally understood it, their liturgy does not merely approach or reflect upon all this from without, nor does it merely circle this mystery from a distant orbit. Rather, Christians have traditionally understood their liturgical efforts to be somehow enacting the mystery itself, locking together its divine and human agents in a graced commerce, the effective symbol of which is that communion between God and our race rooted in the union of divine and human natures in Christ Jesus. In the incarnation, God welds himself to us, and us to himself, without confusion. In Christ Jesus, God becomes like us in all things except our sin. In the liturgy, God welds himself into our media of discourse without becoming subordinate either to those media or to us who must use them. Christian tradition knows that God is not restricted to a sacramental order or to rite, but he has nevertheless willed to work through these media regularly as nowhere else in creation because it is precisely in these that we work upon ourselves and construct our world. It was into these media that we introduced the snake by our sin. It is in the thick of these media that God in Christ seeks the snake out.

There is nothing arbitrary or arcane in any of this unless, perhaps, one ignores the presence of sin in the world and exculpates us from being its author. God in Christ is constrained by our free choice to sin, our happy fault, and sets about saving us at the exact point where we choose to stray, that is, in the disorder and chaos our free will introduces into our world-making. The world we choose to create for ourselves is where:

"The chill ascends from feet to knees,
the fever sings in mental wires.
If to be warmed, then I must freeze
And quake in purgatorial fires
Of which the flame is roses, and the smoke is briars.

The dripping blood our only drink,
The bloody flesh our only food:
In spite of which we like to think
That we are sound, substantial flesh and blood—
Again, in spite of that, we call this Friday good."[39]

Chapter Seven

Liturgy, Canonicity, and Eschatology

The taxonomy of liturgy begun in the preceding
chapter was undertaken in view of liturgy's final end,
God. Beginning in this way may help one to see that
the God who needs neither liturgy nor rite gave us
orthodoxia not merely because he knows what is good
for us, but because in our misuse of these two
inventions of our own we distort the world. Similarly,
the God who needs no words gave us the Word not
merely because he knows he must communicate with
us in ways we can understand, but because in our
misuse of language, an invention of our own, we fatally
distort the world. Both liturgy and Word are called
divine by Christians not because God is ultimate author
of either, but because liturgy and Word, to a degree
unique among all other human media of
communication, have God's own presence at their core
every time they are enacted. Neither liturgy nor Word
can of themselves, therefore, lead the People who use
them into those fatal pathologies which other human
media lead people into. Liturgy and Word lead us
inexorably home, and they do so *with* the grain of our
own free will rather than against it. We remain free to
wander off and lose ourselves if we wish. A liturgy and
a Word called divine cannot, however, be party to this;
both stand, like lighthouses, as a judgment upon
whether and to what extent we depart willfully from
the One who abides gracefully as Friend and Host
within the table fellowship of the assembly which

proclaims the Word and enacts the liturgy called divine. Neither Word nor liturgy of the Word are adiaphora about God. Both together are the foundational form the grace of God takes when it works itself out within our social midst. Liturgy no less than Word is of God.

Only on this basis can the *lex supplicandi* be said to found and constitute the *lex credendi*. Only on this same basis can the liturgy be said to represent regularly and dependably the ordinary way in which the Church teaches from day to day, week to week, year to year, generation to generation, century to century; this is why this sort of *didascalia* or teaching takes precedence over the extraordinary teaching of bishops and councils, and over the secondary teachings of theologians. Such individuals, no matter what their rank, charism, or ability, are themselves nurtured constantly by the divine Presence encountered worshipfully in the assembly of their peers in faith. The liturgy produces them; they do not produce it. The language of worship mediates the substance on which bishops, councils, and theologians reflect. Without that substance, their sort of theology would have no referent.[40]

Whatever else that substance may be said to be, when mediated by liturgy on the deepest foundational level it is not words or concepts but the existential reality of a relationship—communion with God in Christ and, therein, with all God's holy people and holy things (which is what *communio sanctorum* means and where the notion stems from). But to say, as Wainwright does, that the liturgy mediates this substance in language which is "religious," as distinct from the truly "theological" language of secondary theologians, is misleading.[41] The language of liturgy is not just religious rhetoric in need of disciplining by the scientific rigor of secondary theology. The language of liturgy is indeed "religious," but it is a "religious" language which is in fact a theological lingo in its own right, a primary *theological language* different from, but architectonic of, the language of theologians. Liturgical language does not relate to the language of theologians as matter relates to form, as is implied when Wainwright makes the reasoning of theologians architectonic and "critical" with respect to liturgy. This move enables him then to claim a special doxological quality for the second-order activity of theology at its own level. Wainwright thinks that this is what Eastern Christianity means when it says that the true theologian is a person who prays. But the dictum, so far from endowing a doxological quality upon the second-order activity of theology, in fact confers a theological quality upon the first-order activity of people at worship. More specifically, the *theologos* in this Eastern dictum is not the scholar in his study but the ascetic in his cell, and the *theologia* implied is not secondary theological reasoning but contemplation on the highest level, the roots of which are sunk deep in the ascetic's own fasting and prayer, particularly in the recitation of the psalter. The "theologian" in this Eastern view is a contemplative whose life is suffused with the *leitourgia* of a cosmos restored to communion in its trinitarian Source. "Theology" is contemplation of God in and for his own sake. Prayer is the condition of this, and prayer, as Evagrius of Pontus said, is the rejection of concepts.[42]

As much as I am indebted to Wainwright's elegant, erudite, and ecumenically sensitive book,[43] it is a work full in the tradition of a particular Reformed kind of western systematic theology which continues to have difficulty in dealing with liturgy as more than a body of religious language needing the help of secondary theological discipline in order to remain consistent, correct, and conceptually orthodox. The difficulty leads

124

to a certain disjunctiveness between the law of worship and the law of belief. The two are perceived in tension rather than in conjunctive complementarity. The two laws become "tags" once the verb *statuat* is removed from the sentence in which the two phrases were originally joined.

It is thus hard for Wainwright to see how absolute certainty could attach to any doctrinal conclusion drawn from the worship of the Church.[44] Absolute certainty is a rather large order to expect of any conclusion, doctrinal or otherwise, drawn from anywhere. The lives of people rarely wait on such certainty before proceeding to the business at hand. To expect that the worship life of faithful people will yield up absolute doctrinal certainty seems to expect a lot from lives which do not themselves, whether in worship or out of it, move to absolute certainty on any or all matters human or divine. The lives of real people, it seems, move less according to absolute certainties than according to what Peter Berger and others have called structures of plausibility knit together by an overarching "sacred canopy" of sanctioned, if not always or ever absolute and demonstrable, certainties.[45] Given the human nature of liturgical engagement, even under grace, one is free to doubt that a kind of essentialist epistemology which must speak in terms of *absolute* certainty rather than in terms of plausibility and *functional* certainties can avoid warping one's grasp of what liturgy really is and how it actually functions.

A people's liturgy, like the people themselves, does not wait upon absolute certainty. It, like them, takes risks, even faith risks, because plausibility, unlike absolute certainty, is rife with risk. Standing before the living God is a risky business. People dare to do so not because they are irrational but because they have found it plausible that they, like others before them (even Moses), might do so without actually being incinerated, and that the advantages of doing so outweigh the disadvantages of not doing so, the deity remaining all the while alarmingly unpredictable. Whom God loves he chastises. It is risky to sit at the Lord's table, and there is absolutely no certainty that one will not end up on it with one's own body broken, one's own blood poured out. But it is plausible in faith that one might risk the whole thing and even be the better for it. That so many others before have taken the risk and turned out the better for it is a constant awareness which throws, so to speak, a sacred canopy of functional rather than absolute certainty over the entire endeavor. The same holds true for a Christian people's risking prayer to any saint or celebration of the bodily assumption into heaven of her whom they have persisted, daringly, in calling the Mother of God.

The liturgy is neither structured nor does it operate in such a way as to provide doctrinal conclusions. These are distilled from the liturgy by theologians according to the general principle that data are not *given* but must be consciously *taken*. Doctrinal conclusions are lifted from the liturgical engagement of Christians by theologians whose consciousness at the time of the lifting ineluctably affects what is lifted. This means that doctrinal conclusions are selective and may well tell one more about the theologian, and about the state of theological discourse at the time the conclusions are taken, than about the liturgy itself. The process is tactical; for this reason alone it is dubious that a strategic "absolute certainty," which would have to be and remain valid in all circumstances thereafter, could attach to such conclusions. The unlikeliness of this happening, it must be noticed, is a comment on the *process* by which conclusions are reached rather than on the liturgy itself, which abounds in "certainties" of various sorts whether theologians take them or not. The liturgy, like nature, does not exist for the sake of being analyzed by experts, despite the fact that experts can and do analyze both. Nor can doctrinal conclusions be taken from the worship of the Church in general, because this is something which has been rendered universal and abstract by the lifting process itself and thus falsified *a priori*. Ptolemy, working from a similar notion of nature-in-general, drew conclusions concerning the astronomical movements of heavenly bodies which appeared at the time to be absolutely certain. Only later, after centuries of experiments with nature in specific, was the Ptolemaic system shown to be in serious error. Recalling this makes it easier to appreciate that the liturgy, like nature, is never abstract in the real order but always conditioned by era, culture, language, and its human agents' perception of God's presence in their midst.

Perhaps the lesson to be learned from all this is that our modern quest for meaning is a riskier and more inconclusive business than we usually think it is, especially when we equate what something means with the analytical or interpretative process by which a meaning we can recognize is distilled. When secondary theologians go after the meaning of something called the worship of the Church in this manner, it is fairly certain that only certain sorts of data will be taken consciously, and that these data themselves will invariably be rendered universal and abstract as a result of the very process by which the data are taken. Having been universalized, the body of data can then be used as a criterion for authentic meaning against which diverse expressions in a variety of liturgical rites can be measured. In this way, secondary theology comes to control worship by determining *a priori* what its authentic meaning is to be. The historic variety of liturgical usages East and West is thus collapsed into a single noetic paradigm. Whatever runs beyond or contrary to this paradigm becomes a datum which cannot be taken, an insignificant deviant which may be deplored, ignored, or (which is more likely) misinterpreted. Comparative study of liturgical usages is thus unnecessary, thanks to secondary theology which, like the Ptolemaic system, is able to account for Christian worship as a whole without recourse to specific analysis of concrete systems and agencies. A Byzantine *kontakion*, a Gallican *contestatio*, a Roman *oratio*, a Lutheran *chorale*, and even an Indian *sutra* all mean the same thing—only the style, which is of little consequence since it is not about meaning, being different.

The trouble with this sort of thing is that it contains a grain of truth while remaining blind to the fact that it is by no means the whole truth. The grain of truth is that fundamental experience is often common in our race, and its expression may well take on different forms from religious culture to religious culture both outside and inside Christianity. More frequently than not, however, it takes careful analysis to be able to say with certainty which fundamental human experience is in fact being expressed in a given form such as a prayer, hymn, or *sutra*. Even when this is accurately determined, moreover, it is a further question whether the fundamental experience is completely univocal in all societies which give it expression. For example, is the fundamental human experience of death exactly the same for a Buddhist on the one hand and an Orthodox or Catholic Christian on the other? Does it make no real fundamental difference that for the first death is a step into the great void, that for the second it is personal participation in the resurrection to new life of him who is believed to have "trampled death by his death"? If there is no real difference between the two, then Buddhist *sutra* and Byzantine *troparion* are indeed saying the same thing. But if there is a difference between the two, then *sutra* and *troparion* are not saying the same thing, and to suggest that they are is at best a misleading exercise in equivocation. *Sutra* and *troparion* have their own valuable insights to offer concerning a fundamental human experience, but to collapse these insights in upon each other makes almost certain that the insights specific in both will be occluded and misperceived.

This issue is central when it comes to studying Christian liturgy by comparing different liturgical systems. These systems amount to different forms of expression of the fundamental Christian experience. More important than even this, they are systems in which faith is transacted in ways which are different from each other. Some differ from others only slightly, like regional accents of one and the same language. Some differ more, like dialects of a common language. Others differ significantly, like English differs from German and Greek while all three remain members of the one Indo-European family of languages. Christian liturgical systems are thus constituent parts of Christian world views and faith views which, although related, may differ widely. The implications of this for the study of Christian liturgy are serious and far-reaching, especially as they touch the method by which such a study should best be carried on.

Robert Taft, in an essay already referred to,[46] points out that there is no communication without clarity, no clarity without understanding, no understanding without organization, and organization means system. Structural linguistics, for example, attempts to set up unified systems, or "intelligibility structures," in order to clarify the structure and basic laws of how language works. This helps teachers to instruct students about what a verb is. On a more sophisticated level, it aids experts to reverse the process from system building to language reconstruction so that extinct languages can be reconstituted from their surviving fragments. What the anthropologist Claude Lévi-Strauss calls the "surface structure" may vary from language to language, but the "deep structure" is largely common. And commonality is the basis of all generalization, the prerequisite of all system.

As Lévi-Strauss applied this sort of analysis to the study of systems of myth, Taft thinks it can also be applied *mutatis mutandis* to the study of liturgy. Liturgies have "surface structures" which vary; they also have "deep structures" which are common. Both methods are comparative. Each seeks the deep commonality underlying all individual differences that permits systematization.

But where the structuralist seeks meaning, Taft thinks, the liturgical scholar seeks primarily *the structure itself*. For in the history of liturgical development, structure more often than not outlives meaning. Elements endure even after their original meaning has shifted or is lost, or when those same elements become detached from their original limited place and purpose, picking up new and broader meanings in the process. Sometimes new elements are introduced which have no apparent relationship to others. Determining what the basic structure has been, and what its fate has been at crucial points in the evolutionary process, is the primary goal of liturgical research before questions of meaning can be addressed adequately.

In the history of liturgical explanation, however, symbolic or theological interpretation has been given primacy over structural analysis. From at least the time of Amalarius of Metz in the ninth century, western liturgical commentators have attended mainly to meaning, and their interpretations often have done violence to structure. At periods of neuralgic polemic, as in the sixteenth century and after, liturgical structure was bent to serve theological interpretation. Sound liturgical scholarship today attempts to reverse this sequence, insisting with the structuralists on the primary importance of analysis of the structure itself before relating it to other disciplines such as history, sociology, or theology. These latter disciplines may be crucial for explaining how and why, but prior structural analysis is necessary in recovering the what.

Taft notes further that the purpose of sound method in liturgical studies should be to understand the structure and how it works on its own terms, no matter how others may think it does work or ought to work. He also points out that it is not so much from the accumulation of new data but from the invention of workable systems, or "intelligibility frameworks," that understanding in general advances. So far as the study of liturgy is concerned, this cannot occur through ignorance of history, history being a science not of past happenings but of present understanding of what happened in the past. History is not merely events. It is events which have become ideas or perceptions, and these are of the present. "The past does not change, but we do, which is why the work of history is always of the present and never done."[47] Liturgical history does not deal with the past, therefore, but with tradition, and tradition is a "genetic vision of the present," a present conditioned by the way in which it understands its roots. The purpose of history is not to recover the past, which is impossible, much less to imitate it, which would be fatuous. The purpose of doing liturgical history is to understand present liturgy, which, because it has a history, can only properly be understood in motion, just as the only way to understand a top is to spin it.[48]

This should cause those who study liturgy, in particular secondary theologians who would interpret it, to be cautious of facile and often quite static generalizations about something called *the* liturgy of *the* Church. One cannot spin a top in general, but only in specific. One may doubt, for example, that the role of Christ—or of the Holy Spirit, or of Mary—in *the* worship of *the* Church arises from exactly the same concerns and functions in exactly the same way in Antiochene Syria or Byzantine Constantinople as it does in Roman Italy or the Latin West, not to say in Calvin's Geneva, Lutheran Brandenburg, or Anglican Canterbury. And if one is free to doubt this, one may also doubt that the liturgies of Christians all function in respect of doctrine in all churches in exactly the same way in either the past or the present. The liturgy of a church which has never developed a secondary theology to speak of, such as the Oriental Orthodox Church of Ethiopia or a Pentecostal church in America, obviously cannot function in respect of doctrine in the same way as the liturgy of a church which has developed such a secondary theology, especially a church in which secondary theology has become primary.

The fact is that when one lies far enough offshore to see the whole worship of the whole Church, one sees only towers and steeples which merge in the distance. One cannot see how different they are. Some towers belong to churches, some steeples to television stations. Some have bells in them, others soldiers on watch. Even less can one see that these buildings stand in different towns, some even in different countries. People with different pasts, languages, ethnic origins, and cultures mill about at their bases doing different things, living in different ways, venerating different images, upholding different values. What one sees are surface structures which great distance makes to seem the same when they are not. What one cannot see are the deep structures which make all the difference when it comes to distilling that commonality which is the basis of all generalization, the prerequisite of all system, even for

132

secondary theologians who attempt a systematic theology of *the* worship of *the* Church.

It is not enough to attend to meaning apart from structural analysis. Meaning is notoriously malleable according to *a prioris* which are often hidden. Meaning can be, has been, and is applied regularly to liturgy from without, the result being that liturgy is called upon to answer questions it has not posed, to engage in debates in which it has no part. Being found wanting before such demands, the liturgy then is dismissed as having nothing to say, or is altered so as to give it something to say to such questions in such contexts.

When my generation was taught the tract on the eucharist in Catholic seminaries before the Second Vatican Council, for example, we were in fact taught not about the eucharist as an act of worship but about the real presence of Christ which valid and licit confection of the sacrament could be expected to produce by minimal observance of the rite. No eucharistic text was cited except for the words of institution, together with commentaries on these words by secondary theologians who were responding to Protestant denials of the real presence as medieval and counter-reformation Catholics understood it. We were taught little of substance about baptism, even less about its deep structural relationship with the eucharist in the initiatory act which constitutes both a Christian and the Church as the Body corporate of Jesus Christ. We were not exposed to any liturgical history, our liturgical story, much less to the tradition, that genetic vision of the present conditioned by the present's understanding of its roots. We were instructed only in the conventionalities of current theological debates. We were thus left innocent of history, untouched by liturgical understanding, bereft of the tradition's genetic vision of the present. We were left fat from a diet replete with interpretative meaning. But we were never taught the rigors of fasting through the patient austerities of structural analysis and comparative study of liturgical history.[49] We learned interpretation of a sort, but we never knew fully what was being interpreted. Allow me to illustrate what I mean by this.

In the context of eucharistic polemic, we were taught that, because the *lex supplicandi* constitutes the *lex credendi,* and because Catholics had Benediction of Blessed Sacrament, therefore the Catholic doctrine of the real presence of Jesus Christ in the Sacrament by transubstantiation was constituted as part of the *lex credendi.* This is what was called an argument from the liturgical practice of the Church. While the argument was not exactly fallacious, its premises could hardly be said to support entirely the conclusions arrived at. Vastly more serious, however, was the narrow and superficial understanding of *lex supplicandi* betrayed by this sort of argument, an understanding which further narrowed or even falsified the law's relationship to the *lex credendi* and greatly oversimplified the traditional articulation between them both. *Lex supplicandi* is something much more specific than the broad and fuzzy notion of the "practice of the Church." While it does indeed have to do with Church worship, at root it has to do with a definite aspect of that worship. It is a law of supplicatory prayer—not prayer or worship in general, but of prayer which petitions God for the whole range of human needs in specific, a law of euchological petition. This is the nub of the reason why the *lex supplicandi* founds and constitutes the *lex credendi* and is therefore primary for Christian theology. The way Christians believe is, somehow, constituted and supported by how Christians petition God for their human needs in worship.

The reason why this is so seems to be rooted in what happens to one in baptism. If by faith and baptism a Christian is associated intimately with the risen Christ,

134

then the Christian has been graced so as to stand with him, the great High Priest who has entered into heaven itself, now to appear in the presence of God on our behalf (Hebrews 9:24), petitioning his Father for the world. In liturgical tradition, the very first thing a new member of Christ does after baptism is to join with the rest of the baptized in their *supplicatio* before God in Christ for the world, that is, in the great priestly Prayers of the Faithful. This must be done before the eucharist can begin.[50] It is a major priestly act of reconciliation with God in Christ, so much so that whether done in bidding or litanic form it terminates in the kiss of peace exchanged among the members of Christ who have just prayed it in him.

The *lex supplicandi* here takes on concrete euchological form whose *raison d'être* is the baptized status of those who, in Christ, pray in such a way. The sources of the worship tradition consistently pinpoint the very first act of worship of a newly baptized Christian to be supplicatory petition, a form of prayer which also occurs regularly within that other great form of Christian prayer, the prayer of eucharistic thanksgiving itself—in the epiclesis petition (whether in pneumatic form or not) and in the petitions for world and Church which regularly unfold out of the epiclesis in some Rites or precede it in others. *Lex supplicandi* thus has primary reference to a particular type of Christian prayer, and then by extension it can be referred to the broader spectrum of liturgical worship in general. But when it is extended even farther to encompass the whole "practice of the Church," liturgical or not, the law begins to lose both focus and force, and to be applied problematically.

All this suggests that liturgical theology, as distinct from other sorts of theology which may be about the liturgy, is obliged to begin and end with an accurate perception of what a liturgy is in itself, and of how a liturgy functions within the larger context of what I have called rite. Fundamental to this perception is that liturgy is worship of God corporately as church. And since a church is a society if it is anything, all the patterns and structures of human social behavior come into play when Christians assemble for liturgical worship.

Erving Goffman has pointed out that there are three general types of social relationships among people.[51] The first is the *one-to-one* relationship found between parent and child, between lovers, between friends. This type of relationship is intense and tends toward exclusivity. It is not the social relationship that liturgical worship is, although it is often found under certain conditions to be included within that larger and more complex relationship.

A second type of social relationship is that of *one to many*, as is found in a lecture situation where one speaker addresses a group. This relationship may be more or less intense, its active agent a single individual or a corporate individual such as a choir or orchestra performing in symphony before an audience. Some worship spaces, such as the preaching hall with prominent pulpit as the main focal point with ranks of pews in front of it, imply that Christian worship is based on a social relationship of one to many, of a learned ordained person to a congregation of unordained and probably unlearned people. This relationship could hardly be more hieratic, but its spatial expression is both relatively rare and definitely late in the architectural history of Christianity, and its presence denotes a form of worship which was designed to be nonliturgical on purpose.

Liturgical worship is based on a third type of social relationship which Goffman calls that of *many to many*.

136

It is found most often in what he designates "social occasions," as at parties, dinners, political conventions, and celebratory events in which a complex mutuality of presences overlap, compenetrate, and are shared more or less simultaneously. Four things should be noticed about such a "social occasion." First, it is *occasional*, not in the sense that it is irregular or rare but that it is a very special sort of event no matter how often or seldom it happens. Second, due to the very complexity of its mutuality of presences it is *formal*. This means that it has to have rules which are usually extensive and heavily sanctioned by the social group which engages in it. A mother who falls asleep while nursing her child is one thing. A student who nods off during a lecture is another. But one who naps during the soup course at a banquet will bear a burden of public sanction the other two will not. One behaves and dresses differently for a drink with a friend than one does for a state dinner or a formal reception. Third, a "social occasion," due to its formality, is invariably *filled with repetition and that organization of repetition called rhythm*. Dancing and music go together with festivity because both enable a complex mutuality of diverse presences to be shared easily, briefly, and without the group-sundering effort of developing primary one-to-one relationships with everyone with whom one is thrown in contact. Repetition and rhythm become patterns which help secure the mutuality of the group, aiding individuals to relate, cohere, become one within a totality of presences which is greater than its parts. A certain unitary social transcendence is achieved which liberates from the restrictions of individuality. Alienation is reduced and at least briefly overcome. Fourth, the cohesion which results in a "social occasion" is *an effective symbol of social survival*. Societies which cannot cohere on a level which transcends individuality will not long remain either human or social.

No liturgical theology can afford to ignore the basic
facts that the "social occasion" which is a liturgical act
is occasional, formal, unifying, and about survival.
These basic facts help to throw some light not only on
the liturgy's deep structures, but on the underlying
congruity between the several disciplines embraced by
the study of liturgy, including the discipline of liturgical
theology.

That a "social occasion" is occasional, for example,
suggests that liturgy is *festive*. It is a very special event
no matter how often or how seldom it happens.
Liturgy's festivity involves it necessarily in the details
of time and season, details which require calculations
and calendars. These are what the discipline of
heortology, the study of feasts and seasons, deals
with.[52]

That a "social occasion" is formal means that liturgy
has a certain *order* of procedure about it. It is this
specific order which distinguishes Christian baptism
from all other forms of human bathing, which marks
off Christian eucharist from all other forms of human
dining. Its order gives specific form to liturgical
structure and differentiates Christian liturgical behavior
from all other similar forms of human ritual behavior,
while the same order relates liturgical behavior to all
those other forms as well.[53] Studying the origins,
growth, and comparison of liturgical orders, and
analyzing their individual structures, is the main
burden of *historical studies* of the liturgy.[54] These are
concerned primarily with *what* will be the subject of
subsequent investigations into the *why* of liturgical
growth and the *how* of liturgical modulation in a given
era, including one's own.

That a "social occasion" is repetitious and rhythmic
suggests that liturgy is necessarily enmeshed in space
and time. Worship in Spirit and in truth is never

abstract, nor does it happen on some noetic level which is undifferentiated like a Cartesian grid.[55] Liturgy happens only in the rough and tumbled landscape of spaces and times which people discover and quarry for meaning in their lives. This is an *artistic* enterprise. Liturgical repetition is thus a knowledgeable accomplishment, and its organization into definite rhythms of sounds, sights, gestures, and even smells is an act of human artistry—no more nor less so than building a house, composing a concerto, laying out a town, or playing cello. Therefore the student of liturgy must know not only heortology and history but the spatial, sonic, visual, and kinetic arts of ceremonial choreography as well. A liturgical scholar who is illiterate in the several human arts can never know his or her subject adequately. To this extent, such a one will inevitably report the liturgy to secondary theologians in a manner more or less warped.

That a "social occasion" is repetitious and rhythmic means also that liturgy is *unifying,* for repetition and rhythm have this effect upon human assemblies for worse or better. The unity which repetition and rhythm produce in social gatherings is so power-laden as to be a matter of concern. It can be so powerful as to drive a mob to violence under the orchestration of a demagogue. It may attain monstrous proportions, as at a Nazi *Parteitag* in Nuremberg. But *koinonia,* the unity of the churches of God, may be its result as well. To assure the latter and rule out the former is the main reason why Christian *orthodoxia* has always been *canonical,* which means that it is governed by rule or *kanon.* The liturgy's canonicity goes beyond the rules of formality and aesthetics. Nor is there only a single rule or canon governing liturgy. There are several canons, all of which compenetrate and interact to assure, insofar as canons may, that the liturgy of Christians does not drift into delusion and fantasy but remains worship in Spirit and in truth. Each of the several canons is the result of innumerable complex transactions carried on within the worshipping assembly itself over considerable periods of time.

First, there is the *canon of holy scripture*. This canon governs what the assembly deems appropriate that it should read and hear as it stands before God in worship. It is this special existential stance with respect to the divine Presence which constrains the assembly's choice to those written works which bespeak authentically that Presence to save in the world. For this reason, the canon of holy scripture embraces written works not for their literary merit nor on the basis of the piety of their authors, but on the grounds of their being "of God" rather than just "about God." It is only with great caution that the liturgy makes use of any other written compositions in its order of service, and even then it is the close proximity of these written works to the canonical scriptures which recommends them far more than their stylistic quality or the interest of their contents. Of all the canons which affect liturgical worship, it is the canon of holy scripture which keeps the assembly locked into the fundamental relationship that gives it its unique character among all other human gatherings, namely, its relationship to the presence in its midst of the living God.

Second, there is the *canon of baptismal faith* summed up in the several trinitarian creeds.[56] The earliest of these grew out of the three questions put to candidates for baptism as they stood naked in the font concerning their faith in Father, Son, and Holy Spirit. The creeds thus distill the substance of revealed Gospel into baptismal form precisely at the instant when membership is consummated in the corporate person of him whose Gospel it is. Next to the canon of holy scripture, the credal canon of baptismal faith keeps the assembly's worship firmly rooted in relationship to a divine Presence which is not only vertiginous but communitarian and personal. The creed affirms the assembly's awareness that the living God before whom it stands in worship is a community of Persons which wills to manifest itself in the world through a community of human persons wholly devoted to the world's restoration in its Trinitarian Source. The canon of baptismal faith thus constrains the assembly to worship in such a way that its apostolate in the world as icon of the Holy Trinity and agent under God of the world's communion with its Source is rendered accessible to those of good will. The canon checks any temptation the assembly may be under to withdraw into itself and to worship with self-complacency. The canon of baptismal faith cautions ministers not to regard the assembly of the baptized as a clergy support group. It cautions the assembly never to forget that it is nothing less than a chosen race, a royal priesthood, a holy nation, God's own people who exist to declare the wonderful deeds of him who has called it out of darkness into his marvelous light (1 Peter 2:9).

Third, there is the *canon of eucharistic faith* which is carried in the assembly's repertoire of eucharistic prayers or "canons of the Mass." These prayers distill the substance of revealed Gospel and its baptismal creeds into strictly euchological forms of thanksgiving and petition within the corporate person of him whose Gospel is in motion for the life of the world. As the trinitarian questions generate the creed in baptism, so eucharistic prayers generate a euchological "creed" appropriate to the Banquet of the Lamb. For this reason, the eucharistic prayer must be taken as seriously in its own context as the creed must be taken in baptism, and as holy scripture must be taken in the general life of the Church.

Fourth, there is that body of *canonical laws* which regulate the daily living and the due processes of assemblies of Christians in conformity with the foregoing canons of scripture, creed, and prayer. Canonical laws, which are often denigrated as being unimportant, attempt to render the other three canons specific in the small details of faithful daily life. When canonical laws are overlooked too long, the other three canons are likely to drift away from a church's consciousness and to be honored only in the breach. When this happens, such a church will invariably discover its apostolate to be compromised, its faith dubious, its worship more concerned with current events than with the presence of the living God, and its efforts bent more to maintaining its own coherence than to restoring the unity of the world to God in Christ.

Finally, that a "social occasion" is about survival suggests that liturgy has an *eschatological dimension* throughout, even when its surface structures may seem to be concerned overtly with a historical commemoration (such as the day of Jesus' death) or a current event. But liturgy's deep structures always betray the continuing awareness of the faithful that the One in whose presence they stand is beyond time and time's end no less than time's beginning, Alpha and Omega. Thus even when the liturgy of Christians deals with time, as it inevitably must, it does so not in the short term but *sub specie aeternitatis*, that is, eschatologically.[57]

The liturgy is thus festive, ordered, and accomplished through a variety of artistic media. It is possible, even appropriate, that the disciplines of heortology, ritual history, and the study of the several liturgial arts be carried on according to methodologies which are not themselves theological. It does not seem possible, however, to deal with liturgy's canonical aspect, or with the eschatological dimension one meets within its deep structures, without entering into strictly theological discourse. For liturgical canonicity and eschatology are functions of that theological awareness which is native to the liturgical assembly itself. Liturgical canonicity and eschatology are, moreover, primary symptoms of that change, already mentioned, which occurs in the assembly of faithful people as they encounter the divine Presence in their act of liturgical worship. When Christians adjust to the change in them which God causes regularly in their liturgical worship, the adjustment is normally reflective and critical in terms of the four canons governing their corporate life *in the present,* and also in terms of their ultimate survival *in an eschatological future* which is already being worked out in them by God's grace and their own cooperation with that grace by faith and works. This is what it means to say that the liturgical act of Christians is not merely a mine from which scholars may dig material for second-order theological constructions. Nor is the liturgy just a dictionary from which the learned derive terms with which to write second-order theological treatises. Rather, the liturgy of faithful Christians is the primary theological act of the Church itself, and the ways in which this primary theological act carries on its own proper discourse are couched in terms of canonicity of content and structure, and in terms of eschatological survival.

When one comes to describe a liturgical theology, as distinct from a systematic theology of the liturgy, the description might be something like this. A liturgical theology is doxological due to the liturgy's festal quality. It is historical due to the liturgy's formal and ordered qualities. It requires critique of the sonic, visual, spatial, and kinetic arts due to the liturgy's immersion in space and time. It involves disciplined reflection on the present and actual state of life in the faithful assembly due to the liturgy's quality of canonicity—which means that a liturgical theology is inherently pastoral. And it involves no less disciplined reflection on the assembly's future discharge of its obligations in service as a corporate ministry of reconciliation according to grace and promise due to the liturgy's eschatological quality—which implies an ecclesiology no less ministerial than it is eschatological and pneumatic. The canonical "now" and the eschatological "future" frame *orthodoxia* as a life of sustained "right worship" in truth and in a Spirit who is not only consolation but promise as well.

Such a description puts liturgical theology beyond socio-anthropological studies of ritual[58] and suggests that it is the result of a whole range of disciplines, not all of which are strictly theological. Nor is it a description of any systematic theology with which I am familiar. A systematic theology may, for example, be said to be "doxological" in a more or less indirect sense, but it does not deal in *doxologia* as does a liturgical theology which is directly rooted in festivity. A systematic theology may be said to be "historical," but when it addresses the liturgy's formal and ordered development in time, it tends to regard liturgical form and order as a set of sources drawn for the most part from the textual surface structures of the liturgy and bereft of the structural and comparative analyses about which Robert Taft writes. But these analyses are as essential here as they are in linguistics if one is to attain to the deep structures where one finds the commonality which is the basis of all generalization, the prerequisite of all system. Without such analysis, the systematician is left with only the differences apparent in surface structures, or with only apparent samenesses in the same structures, and is therefore apt to offer dubious interpretations of "how" and "why" concerning a "what" to which the systematician has

144

little or no access. Such a theology as this rarely mounts a critical evaluation of the sonic, visual, spatial, and kinetic arts in worship, being content to allow others to do this while affirming the arts in general but keeping them out of the theological curriculum. Such a theology is not often found to be very pastoral, and the ecclesiology undergirding it is usually more christic and institutional than ministerial, eschatological, and pneumatic.

This is in no way to denigrate the importance of systematic theology. Its advantages are real and many; they have shaped profoundly the whole western intellectual and even spiritual approach to God, so much so that other sorts of approach to God sometimes are made to seem secondary or tertiary if not improper. Yet systematic theology in all its dimensions is neither self-originating nor does it subordinate all other modes of approach to God. Unlike "religious studies," it originates in the fundamental religious experience of faith, and its quest for understanding that experience proceeds by constant recourse to that experience as it continually takes on ecclesial form. Faith, not systematic theology, saves. Faith, not systematic theology, produces the Church. Systematic theology is neither ceremony nor doxology, but systematic theology—something Thomas Aquinas categorized, along with other intellectual pursuits, as a science of second intentions, that is, a discourse of concepts about concepts dialectically advanced by the testing of propositions. He also noted that "the believer's act of faith does not terminate in a proposition, but in a thing. For as in science we do not form propositions except in order to arrive through them at a knowledge of things, so it is in faith."[59] The "thing" about which systematic theology forms propositions is the encounter between God and the world which liturgical rite enacts among those of faith.

It is for this reason, once more, that systematic theology and its scientific analogues are said to be secondary, and their discourse to be second-order language—rather as physics may be said to be secondary, and its discourse to be second-order language. What is primary for systematic theology is the act and elaboration of faith. What is primary for physics is the physical act and its consequences. Although imperfect, as all analogies are, this one may help to make some distinctions in the category of liturgical theology which until now have been only implicit.

I have insisted so far upon the liturgical act as the primary theological act in a church's life because it is the first act of critical reflection triggered by faith-encounters with the presence of the living God in the midst of those who assemble precisely for this end. As such, the liturgical dialectic of encounter, change, and adjustment to change amounts to a reflective *and* lived theology which is native to all the members of the faithful assembly. This is *theologia* which is constant, regular, and inevitable as these people encounter God in worship and adjust to the changes God visits upon them. The liturgical assembly is thus a theological corporation and each of its members a theologian. But the assembly's members are, as such, not secondary theologians, nor is their theological discourse second-order language. Their theological capacity and discourse are nonetheless real for all this, and both lie closer to the reality which is faith than does the theological ability and discourse of those who practice analysis by concept and proposition in a scientific manner. Mrs. Murphy and her pastor do not fail to be theologians at the point where the seminary professor who taught the pastor succeeds in being one. The professor is a secondary theologian. Mrs. Murphy and her pastor are primary theologians whose discourse in faith is carried on not by concepts and propositions nearly so much as in the vastly complex vocabulary of experiences had, prayers said, sights seen, smells smelled, words said and heard and responded to, emotions controlled and released, sins committed and repented, children born and loved ones buried, and in many other ways no one can count or always account for. Their critical and reflective discourse is not merely about faith. It is the very way faith works itself out in the intricacies of human life both individually and in common. Its vocabulary is not precise, concise, or scientific. It is symbolic, aesthetic, ascetical, and sapiential. It is not just something she and her pastor think or say, but something they taste, the air they breathe. It is a sinuous discourse by which they and those innumerable millions like them, dead and born and yet unborn, work out the primary body of perceived data concerning what it really means when God pours himself out into humanity, into the world as a member of our race. Nowhere else can that primary body of perceived data be read so well as in the living tradition of Christian worship.

Here the student of liturgy may be of some modest service in aiding the secondary theologian to read the primary body of perceived data in a living tradition of Christian worship. What needs to be read is rite. Its grammar, vocabulary, and syntax are no less definite than that of the language the secondary theologian already knows. No less definite, but quite different. Nor can it be read as one reads a book or a research paper. It more closely resembles reading a musical score containing bits of libretto and choreographical notations. Vocabulary, grammar, and syntax are represented not in words about concepts but in notes about sounds and movements which are produced actively in order to involve both performer and hearer together in a common experience, a faith encounter, rather than to provide an argument and a conclusion for a reader. A liturgiologist is not unlike a musicologist who attempts to account first for *what* and then for *how* and *why* a composer or a whole school of composers composed the way they did, for what purpose, and with the particular sonic repertoire which is provided by a particular culture's way with sound. Neither musicologist nor liturgiologist are properly performance critics per se. Even less are they conductors, performers, or teachers of performance. For neither liturgy nor music is only a how-to matter. The actual doing of music, no less than of liturgy, is better left to those with the appropriate skills. Liturgiologists, like musicologists, serve best in aiding others to grasp more fully the nature, standards, and dimensions of their endeavors.

A liturgiologist does this best by following the advice of Robert Taft quoted earlier. The liturgiologist must be a master student of liturgical structures and their comparative relationship from one Rite to another. Only thus can he or she establish the *what* which others may further interpret as to the *why* and *how*. The liturgiologist helps others read a score of rite for what it really is. Liturgics, which is the discipline a liturgiologist practices, is thus not a performing art, nor is it a species of something seminary catalogues often call "practical theology." It is a major discipline, similar to biblical exegesis or church history or doctrinal theology, particularly in those institutions which devote themselves to preparing people for ministry to assemblies of faith.

But liturgics is of even broader relevance than this. How one can ever grasp the values and mechanisms by which any human society maintains itself for worse or better is difficult to imagine without a fairly sophisticated notion of how such a society ritualizes itself in daily life. Social rituals constitute the myriad

148

ways in which any society enacts itself, gives itself distinctive form in space and time. But it is those most urgently concerned with social values and maintenance who are usually aphasic about ritual and the first to dismiss ritual as having anything to do with social survival. Societies nonetheless are constantly working out their survival in the intricacies of their formative daily rituals, and the first symptoms of social upheaval or dissolution are always to be found in the breakup or breakdown in a society's daily rituals. When the ritual codes of respect for each other's privacy, of precedence, of regard in naming, and of reverence for the sick and old begin to fade, one may wonder whether egalitarianism and entitlement monies for groups now bereft of anything but political or utilitarian claims will make good the loss. In this perspective, ritual studies in general may be seen as a stethoscope placed on the heart of a human society, and liturgics a stethoscope placed on the heart of a church.

This chapter has attempted to specify further the taxonomy of liturgy itself by calling attention to those qualities it seems to possess in common with any social occasion in which a mutuality of presences is involved. Because every social occasion is unifying and about survival, the social occasion called liturgy appears on its own evidence to be *canonical* and *eschatological*. These two qualities, which root liturgy in the present no less than in the long-term future, are those which particularly affect how primary theology is carried on by those who, beyond ordinary human efforts, live a life of one, holy, catholic, and apostolic "right worship" both inside and outside assemblies of faith. The canonical and eschatological qualities of Christian liturgy are, moreover, the ones which give specifically Christian stamp to the liturgy's being also *festive*, *ordered*, and *critical* as regards the various arts it uses.

On this basis, the chapter claimed that the true primary theologian in the Church is the liturgical assembly in each and every one of its members; that this primary theology is festive, ordered, steeped in the arts, canonical, and eschatological; that this primary discourse is what produces the body of basic faith perceptions upon which secondary theology is nurtured in its normal and healthy state. In this view, *lex supplicandi* and *lex credendi* are not detachable or opposable laws but subtly correlative, the first founding the second, the second affecting (although not founding) the first. Each law functions in concert with the other within the discourse of primary theology. This means that *lex credendi* is at root not merely something which is done exclusively by secondary theologians in their studies, as opposed to *lex supplicandi* done by nontheologians indulging in religious worship elsewhere. On the contrary, *lex credendi* is constantly being worked out, sustained, and established as the faithful in assembly are constantly working out, sustaining, and establishing their *lex supplicandi* from one festive, ordered, aesthetic, canonical, and eschatological liturgical act to the next under grace. *Lex credendi* is always in reality joined to *lex supplicandi* by an active verb as object is joined to subject, and the resulting affirmation says something central about primary theology and the relation of secondary theology to it. *Lex supplicandi legem statuat credendi* thus says something about the deepest structure and purpose of Christian worship. It also suggests a method of analytical procedure which the secondary theologian ignores to the Church's peril. For the liturgy of faithful Christians is the primary theological act of the Church itself, and the ways in which this act carries on its proper discourse are above all canonical in structure and content, and eschatological in intent.

150

Chapter Eight

Liturgy and Normality

The preceding three chapters have investigated the possibility of seeing Christian liturgical worship as a constitutive and foundational theological enterprise. And since, according to Mary Douglas, learning and preception depend on classifying and distinguishing,[60] I have investigated the possibility by offering a taxonomy of liturgy mounted from what earlier philosophers would have called its final, formal, and efficient causalities. All this was done against a background of distinction in theology itself as an enterprise carried on in first and second order manners. I have suggested that part of our difficulty in grasping liturgy as a constitutive and foundational enterprise, as distinct from its being little more than ceremonied adiaphora, may lie in our tendency to make secondary theology primary and primary theology secondary.

It now seems appropriate to close off this taxonomy of liturgy by pointing out in specific what liturgy and, by implication, liturgical theology are not. Such a series of negations may bring us close to what is positively normal in each.

Due to its festive nature, for example, liturgy is not ordinary, utilitarian, or for something.[61] Christians do not engage in liturgical worship to get grace or inspiration, to indulge in creativity, to become educated in matters ecclesiastical. Nor do they elaborate rite as a style of life to house nostalgia, to provide rest, to proffer moral uplift, or to supply aesthetic experience. While any or all of these results may accrue to an individual or an assembly as by-products of the liturgical engagement, they constitute neither in whole nor in part the engagement's motive. The feast remains its own end. The business Christians transact in liturgy is festal business because, simply, Christ has conquered death by his death. Liturgical theology is therefore a festal endeavor, a doxological rather than any other sort of enterprise. And it is this in a way and to a degree that sytematic theology, for all its other virtues, is not.

Due to its ordered character, liturgy is no more informal than any other human "social occasion" is without form. The history of Christian worship reveals an evolution of forms and formality to the detriment of makeshift, the idiosyncratic, and the aggressively enthusiastic. As the latter three characteristics turn up, they tend to be resisted by the assembly as a whole and then to be suppressed in one way or another by the assembly's ministers. A case in point may be seen in 1 Corinthians 11–14, where St. Paul cautions a particular church concerning eucharistic disorder which rends the assembly, charismatic enthusiasms which polarize the assembly, and the public behavior of certain women which causes uneasiness in Paul both as a traditional Jew and as an apostle sent to preach the Gospel in as high a degree of its integrity as God's grace and his own weakness would allow. But his chastisement of the church in Corinth for liturgical disorder is for all, male and female alike. These four chapters are the first lecture in Christian history on the abuse of liturgical order. Liturgical theology is always in search of form and evangelical order.

Due to its incarnation, so to speak, in space and time, something which requires an artistic coping with creation in all its aspects, liturgy is not unworldly in that it cares nothing for the demands of matter, space, sound, and movement. Carelessness concerning these things does not produce spontaneity but confusion and anomie, an assembly intolerant of repetition, arhythmic, incoherent, bereft of form, and dissolute. Liturgical theology thus takes the arts very seriously indeed, being not merely appreciative of them, but critical of them all as they are pressed into the service of assemblies of faith.

Due to its canonical form and content, liturgy is not a battlefield of confrontation and divisiveness. The faithful do not assemble to engage in ideological combat with each other or to be rent asunder by competing special interest groups. Rather, they assemble under grace and according to the canons of scripture and creed, prayer and common laws, in order to secure their unity in lived faith transmitted from generation to generation for the life of the world. Liturgical theology's main tools in trade are therefore the canon of scripture, the canon of the baptismal creeds, the canon of eucharistic prayers, and the canonical laws of community life. The liturgical theologian sees the liturgy as the ritual of a Word made flesh for the life of the world, as a ministry of reconciliation between God and all persons and things in Christ. This is worship in Spirit and in truth.

Finally, due to its eschatological intent, liturgy is about nothing less than ultimate, rather than immediate, survival. It is about life forever by grace and promise. Liturgy regards anything less as a trap and a delusion hostile to the Gospel of Jesus Christ. Like the Sabbath, liturgy is for us rather than we for it. But also like the Sabbath, liturgy is for us in that it summons us by revealed Good News home to a Presence, to a life even now of communion in that Presence. To commune with that Presence is to be in at the end and at the center where the world is whole, fresh, and always issuing new from the Father's hand through Christ in the Spirit. Unlike those who believe that Jesus came once long ago and will come again in a future more or less remote, liturgy moves within the abiding Presence of God in Christ, the uncreated creating Word, who fills the whole of time past, present, and to come. Liturgical theology leans far into this eschatological wind, finding there as nowhere else not only grace's motive but its promise of judgment as well. This stance makes the liturgical theologian, like any other orthodox Christian, an unusually wary person who carries on his or her craft with great circumspection in a workshop through which cosmic storms thunder but the candle flame burns without a flicker. Like standing at a pole where everything one can see on all sides lies in only one direction, when standing here everything one can perceive comes already magnetized with infinity and there are no horizons beyond which one cannot see. It is an odd place filled with clouds of witnesses past, present, and to come who are very odd indeed. The liturgy happens in this odd place, and it is where the liturgical theologian works.

This is so because this is where Christian *orthodoxia* takes its normal stance and elaborates the normal way in which it looks upon all that swirls around it. Its stance and regard are highly judgmental because of its awareness of the proximity of the Presence in which it stands. The Presence is no less transcendental for its immanence in the faithful community and in all other things under heaven. The Presence is source of all that is, the first principle of the community and of all else. Because first principles can be known but not demonstrated according to the rules of human logic,[62] Christian *orthodoxia* knows its first principle only by faith, and the divine Presence thus known is radical in the extreme in what it requires of those who gather in such faith. The radicalness of these requirements

154

cannot be overlooked when one asks in what the normality native to Christian *orthodoxia* might consist. Some examples must suffice to illustrate this point.[63]

The treatise *Concerning Baptism* by Basil of Cappadocia (c. 330–379) résumés the teaching of the early Church fathers in general. Basil's family had been Christian for generations and counted among its members, particularly in Basil's own generation (three of whom were bishops), major figures in the Christian community who had intimate contact with other illustrious people such as Gregory Thaumaturgus and Evagrius of Pontus. The sort of baptism Basil knew was of adults and children who were old enough to answer for themselves, and it was celebrated only after a lengthy catechumenate. More surprising for us today, however, is Basil's repeated use of the story of the rich young man to illustrate for the catechumen what is necessary to be a disciple of Christ. One must first obey the commandments. Then one must sell all and follow him, since " . . . whoever of you does not renounce all that he has cannot be my disciple" (Luke 14:33). This attitude becomes the *leitmotiv* of the entire treatise, and it is directed not to monastic ascetics but to all who are made *christoi* by baptism. "Not only should we not endeavor to increase our possessions and to acquire greater gains, as do men of the world, but we should not even lay claim to the property which has already been acquired and is our own. Let us be zealous in giving to the needy . . . including hostile and wicked men also in our acts of kindness."[64] According to the precedent stated in Acts 4:32–37, this was not absolute poverty but the possession of all things in common, from which distribution was to be made according to need—a point made central again in Basil's letters concerning monastic life as a particular form the lives of baptized Christians might well take.[65] Basil's repeated emphasis is upon baptism as requiring a quite radical sort of poverty on the part of all the baptized. For a Christian, baptism makes imperative through its death and rebirth imagery an evangelical poverty which Basil and much of the tradition after him, particularly in the East, regard as normal.

In this perspective, the later Western medieval tendency to constrict such poverty to those in religious orders (along with, it might be added, a tendency to associate the baptismal characteristics noted by the early fathers as rights and glories of all the baptized to those living in religious orders or preparing for ordination in seminaries) betrays a certain ineluctable departure from orthodox normality. And like all such departures, whether slight or grave, this results in the proliferation of other abnormalities, the effect of which is to warp to some degree how the Gospel will be perceived.[66] What might be called orthodox normality for Basil and his colleagues faded into a mere ideal for all, a requirement reduced to a mere counsel. At this point it could begin to be cited in such a way as to relieve all but Christian elites from concerning themselves either with their own appropriation of evangelical poverty or with active and sensitive care of the poor themselves. A first step was thus taken toward creating a systemic proletarian class of the disadvantaged and the disenfranchised in Western society which would become ripe for destructive revolution all through the later Middle Ages even to our own day.

But it is not only by evangelical poverty that orthodox normality has recognized the baptized as set apart from all those who live abnormal lives according to this world which passes. Basil and the tradition he résumés regard it also as a dimension of orthodox normality that the baptized are bound to nonviolence or nonresistance to evil. "Surely we walk in newness of life and achieve a justice more perfect than that of the scribes and pharisees when we obey these words of the Lord: 'It was said of them of old: "An eye for an eye and a tooth for a tooth." But I say to you not to resist evil . . . .' Not only are we to refrain from revenge for offenses first committed against us, . . . but we should show forbearance greater than the offense and show in advance our readiness to sustain other wrongs of equal or even greater gravity."[67] Prior to Basil, Hippolytus (c. 220) refused to admit even to the catechumenate, much less to baptism, those who followed a profession which might require them to kill someone.[68] This requirement of baptism also faded in subsequent centuries—despite the standing maxims on poverty, meekness, the thirst for righteousness, mercy, purity, peacemaking, and being persecuted and reviled which are contained in the Sermon on the Mount (Matthew 5:3f., Luke 6:20f.). Like evangelical poverty, this symptom of orthodox normality encompassed by the tradition against violence shrank to being an expectation of those in religious orders, at least until Bernard of Clairvaux laid down an approving theological rationale for religious orders of Christian warriors in the twelfth century. Here too, it seems that a growing attenuation in the churches' contact with their own baptismal practice has contributed to a blurring of their vision and perception of what orthodox normality rooted in revealed Gospel entails. To recover normality, one must look for "canonical" statements of it in early writers who articulate the tradition flowing straight out of the Gospel, and look for hints of normality's survival, more or less, in later structures and attitudes as memories or as ideals intended for a select few.

But the situation is neither static nor irreversible so long as the assembly of the faithful remains alive to the Presence of the living God. The first symptom of life is the ability to change. Thus some resonances of normality with respect to evangelical poverty among the baptized can be detected in recent baptismal reforms. The Rite of Christian Initiation of Adults (1972), for instance, insists that catechumens must be formed for baptism not only in doctrinal and ritual ways. They must be set into a process of passage from what they have been to what they must become by baptism into Christ. "This transition, which brings with it a progressive change of outlook and morals, should become evident together with its social consequences . . . . Since the Lord in whom [the catechumen] believes is a sign of contradiction, the convert often experiences human divisions and separations . . . ."[69] Similar resonances of normality may be detected on the matter of nonviolence in the American Roman Catholic bishops' pastoral letter concerning nuclear war (1983). And a restoration of the emphasis on the Sunday eucharist in the local church makes this, rather than the priest's own private devotional Mass, once again the normal foundation of Roman Catholic theology of church and eucharist.[70] These resonances of orthodox normality remained familiar fare for western monks, nuns, and other sorts of religious persons. The fact remains, however, that what we have come to regard in many different ways as a theology of religious life was for Basil the Great and the early Christian fathers simply a consequence of everyone's baptism, and the specialties of later religious orders were originally the rights and property of all the baptized.

That secular societies and attitudes attend far more to violence and the amassing of riches in no way renders abnormal orthodoxy's traditional insistence on nonviolence and evangelical poverty for the baptized. Disciples of Jesus Christ have every right, given the historical record of secular society's demonstrable march of folly, to regard the regularization of violence and the lust for wealth as fatal abnormalities which go against the grain of reality itself. *Orthodoxia* has every reason to regard a child dead of war or starved by poverty as anything but normal. It also has every reason to expect that this world will not be able to abolish such horrors if left to its own resources, and that such a world will not accept gladly the resources of God's grace in the effort. The orthodox are justified on the evidence to regard the world's rejection of such help as the greatest abnormality of all. This is why orthodox Christian tradition has steadily perceived baptism as the fundamental separation of the baptized from such a world, and the worship done by the baptized as something not of this world. This is the antithesis of regarding the world with disinterest. It is, rather, to play extremely hard ball with the world by remaining constantly clearheaded about what the world can and cannot do for itself, and about its perennial need for grace and judgment. Christian *orthodoxia* steadily regards the world as abnormal by its own choice. Christian *orthodoxia* steadily regards itself as the world rendered normal in its having been restored to communion with God in Christ by the power of God's Spirit. What a life of Christian "right worship" thus enacts is not for or about a world which passes due to its own radical abnormality; it enacts a world rendered normal which is itself. In doing so, the assembly suffers greatly, as did its Lord, at the hands of systemic abnormality. It baptizes into death; gives thanks over and itself becomes a body broken and blood shed. It is always vulnerable in its normality to the frenzy of the abnormal. Orthodoxy has deep in its innards the old Sanskrit distillation of prehistoric human wisdom, *tat tvam asi*, be what you are, just so. No more, no less. It knows that liturgical movement begins when the alarm clock goes off every morning and that God's mercy and justice never sleep.

In a world which is abnormal not by constitution but by human choice, none of this is easy. Normality is not

159

attained without a fight, is not sustained without constant effort, a blessed rage for order. It can degenerate beneath slothful hands into mushy *laissez-faire* or into an ironbound *status quo*, the one smothering human effort, the other crystallizing it into a pillar of salt which preserves by killing. For this reason, Christian "right worship" must always be filtered through the criteria of God's alarming Word in Christ. For the same reason, orthodox Christian systems of rite have always included—in addition to the myriad particularities of worship, canonical obedience, evangelical and catechetical structures, and particular styles of theological reflection—ascetical and monastic structures as well. For a life of *orthodoxia*, like health, requires constant discipline in its need to sustain normality, not unlike a jeweler requires fire and acid in the purification of precious metals.

By asceticism here, one does not mean giving up candy during Lent, or flagellants and hair shirts. One means something broader, deeper, and harder; a kind of Zen in the art of maintaining a life of "right worship" as the only way to live in the real order. Evagrius of Pontus (+399), who was the first to synthesize the traditional teachings of Christian asceticism, called it *theoria*, contemplation pure and simple, and he identified this with prayer. He also said that its issue is *theologia* of the most sublime kind, and that its home is a lifetime spent going with the grain of God's creation by grace and effort. "The fear of God strengthens faith, my child, and continence in turn strengthens this fear. Patience and hope make [continence] solid beyond all shaking, and they also give birth to *apatheia*. Now this *apatheia* has a child called *agape* who keeps the door to deep knowledge of the created universe. Finally, to this knowledge succeed *theologia* and the supreme beatitude."[71] *Apatheia* is the word Evagrius' disciple John Cassian rendered into Latin as *puritas cordis*, purity of heart, in which form it entered Western spiritual teaching in the monastic rule of Benedict of Nursia.[72]

The ascetic's fundamental contribution to Christian *orthodoxia* as a life of cosmic normality is thus not education or good works, but an exemplary existence kept clean, clear, and free of this world's intense and warping abnormality. It is a life of lucid and abiding clarity which goes with the grain of reality at every point. Charity emerges from such an unbeholden life, a charity which is absolutely requisite in coming to true knowledge of even the created universe by natural reason. Only from such knowledge can there then arise knowledge of God, *theologia*, and the supreme beatitude of seeing and knowing God face to face. This is a life expected of every one of the baptized, whose ultimate end is the same supreme beatitude. It is a life all the baptized share, a life within which the professed ascetic is nothing more or less than a virtuoso who serves the whole community as an exemplar of its own life. The ascetic is simply a stunningly normal person who stands in constant witness to the normality of Christian *orthodoxia* in a world flawed into abnormality by human choice.

This does not mean that Christians and their ascetics are ordinary people; only that they are normal and live normal lives in an abnormal world. So extraordinary are they in their normality that such a world regards them as alien and, like all aliens, invested with peculiar subversive power. The power they have is something endowed upon them by an abnormal world, not something generated or possessed by themselves apart from such a world. Their use of this power is therefore always somewhat ironic and possesses the sort of courage which is native to the bluff, as when Leo the Great confronted Attila the Hun with only the powerless prestige of Old Rome at his back. It was not divisions armed to the teeth that caused Attila to back down but, it seems, their extraordinary absence.

I invoke all this not merely to say a good word for monastic asceticism, which authors since at least the Renaissance have often bewailed as a let and hindrance to authentic Christian living, and which even liturgical scholars have sometimes indicted for having deleterious effects on the course of liturgical development in both East and West. Without resort to special pleading, it has to be noted that there are just too many monks, nuns, and other ascetics littering Christian history who are simply too involved in every aspect of what I have called the phenomenon of rite to be ignored. The various ministries, ordained and unordained, have been infested with them, and whenever significant shifts in the symbiotic relationship between the assembly and culture have occurred, monks, nuns, and other ascetics have been in the thick of evolving new syntheses of rite. The British church was first a Celtic, and then a Roman, monastic church. Monastic also were the central European churches of the Irish and Anglo-Saxon monastic missions. So too was the Russian church later, the churches of Egypt and Syro-Palestine earlier, and the church of Constantinople after the Latin sack of the city in the early thirteenth century. These churches, due to the close relationship which religious ascetics always maintained with those of simple faith and their traditions of folk wisdom, have exhibited historically an astonishing ability at adapting native cultural elements into emerging new idioms of Christian living without succumbing to those elements.

By contrast, churches caught in such shifts at a time when little or no ascetical agency was operative have displayed less ability in resisting pressures to succumb to new cultural elements. These churches, such as those of the sixteenth-century Reform and Counter-

162

Reform, have tended to go defensively rigid by descents into legalism, rubricism, or some form of fundamentalism; or they have tended to dissolve and vanish into the facade of civil religion, becoming "ordinary," native, and largely bereft of that peculiar power for radical good which an abnormal world confers on the alien normality sustained as a hallmark of historic Christian *orthodoxia*. One recalls in this connection the story of a government official who was sent from Constantinople to admonish Basil of Cappadocia concerning what was expected of him politically as a bishop. Basil in turn admonished the official concerning the differing realms of authority of Caesar and Christ. After this tongue lashing the offended official protested that he had never been spoken to in such a manner by any man. "Then, sir," Basil replied, "you have never spoken with a catholic bishop." One also recalls an incident recounted by Peter Brown. "When the citizens of Antioch expected savage punishment after a riot in 387, the imperial commissioners suddenly found their way to the doomed city barred by a group of Syriac-speaking holy men. While these wild figures interceded for the city, and their speeches were translated from Syriac into Greek, the bystanders 'stood around,' wrote a witness, 'and shivered.' "[73]

This forces me to add one final characteristic to the taxonomy of liturgy and to the sort of theology it enacts. Not only is it festive, ordered, aesthetic, canonical, and eschatological. It is also something which seems even more difficult for us moderns to grasp than any of these. It is normal and normative.

From its normality arise not only the liturgy's primacy at the deepest level, but its immense power as well. This power is not the "power of the sacraments" about which conventional claims are made in standard manuals of theology. The power I mean is a power which precedes this latter power as genus precedes species, as root precedes flower. It is, in New Testament terms, *exousia*—literally something which surges up from the very depths of reality, an existential haymaker, so to speak, an all but unspeakable force which locks human consciousness in a grip of steel. It causes one's hair to stand on end, one's flesh to creep. It is what caused the imperial commissioners outside Antioch to stand around and shiver. Rudolf Otto described it as *fascinans et tremendum*, inexorably attractive and repellant all at once, seductive and overpowering, lovely and horrifying. He located its source in the *sacrum*, the Holy,[74] something which orthodox Christian tradition has placed exclusively in God in Christ so that holiness hovers over all claims to power, beauty, goodness, and truth, pointing them all towards God in Christ, the Holy One, as their creative ground and final sanction.[75] It is a Presence who, when asked its name, responds out of a burning bush with the most normal answer conceivable: "I am who I am," *tat tvam asi*. This upended an obscure shepherd into leading his insigificant extended family back to where it was normal for them to be, contrary to the wishes of Egyptians, Canaanites, Philistines, Assyrians, Greeks, and others who had all the best conventional arguments on their side.

It is the same power which enabled a powerless young Jew to set the world of abnormality on its ear by seeming to dismiss all the heroes of Israel with the words, "Before Abraham was, I am"; to dismiss the pretensions of religion and politics with the words, "Render unto Caesar those things that are Caesar's, and to God those things that are God's." He then went about being so disconcertingly normal—healing the ill, telling the truth, feeding the hungry, raising the downcast, stampeding swine, withering fig trees—that systemic abnormality had him put away, as it thought, for keeps. It is the same power which enabled his at first paralyzed followers, clinging only to themselves around a simple table, to walk finally into the jaws of abnormality itself, pulling its teeth and getting themselves chewed up on the way.

I have said that it was no power in itself. It was precisely the absence of all power typical of naked holiness which appeared to systemic abnormality as the greatest *exousia* of all. It is as though the world perceived that the powerlessness of people such as these had begun to strangle its own abnormality and to reach down deep into its own subconsciousness, where there was no defense against the good, the true, and the beautiful except by recourse to sin. The Holy One and those who are made one in him set about changing the world's mind by first seizing the world's imagination through acts of powerlessness. In doing so they tapped in to the most awesome source of power there is. It is the life-force itself, and they gained access to it by throwing their own lives away. They sank back not into programs and policies, bureaucracies and priorities, but into cosmic and pacific normality. They found that in doing so they had come home to the living God, and that living here was a life and a way of power which passes human understanding.

This is the power which precedes the "power of the sacraments" as genus precedes species, as root precedes flower. It is the power which flows when an assembly of the faithful baptized encounters still and again the living God in liturgical worship. It is the power which summons every human being to that assembly by the grace of conversion, the power which judges every member of the assembly by the same grace to renew and deepen his or her state of conversion week in and week out. It is the power which enables convert and assembly to negotiate a sacramental initiation of the former into the latter which leaves each changed as both enter into a state of eucharistic communion—a life and a ritual of change as constantly wrenching as the act of sacrifice always is. Given who we are, deep change is the root and branch of normality, and it can be sustained for the life of the world only by dwelling in the alarming Presence of the Holy One.

Thus the symbolic vehicles of orthodox normality are themselves quite normal things. Oil and water as in a bath, bread and wine as at a dinner among friends, the touch of human hands, a kiss between lovers, benign gestures, words husbanded rather than squandered, smells and sights that speak, sounds of festivity. None of these singly or together come anywhere close to being equal to the unimaginable power unleashed through them as God transacts with the world in the assembly of orthodox Christians. They are powerless in themselves. They bear whatever power they do just as the powerlessness of the assembly of believers bears the same power, that is, by the donation abnormality makes to the alien presence in its midst of cosmic normality when it is encountered as holiness. The usual question abnormality asks is how many divisions Christians have. The only answer Christian normality can give is that it has none. Nowhere has historic Christianity given this answer more consistently and clearly than in the liturgical systems which anchor those various styles of Christian living I have called rite.

There is nothing narrow or irrelevant about any of this unless the Presence to save and the Gospel it reveals are narrow or irrelevant. It is as broad and deep as creation and redemption themselves. Like a superb act of music or poetry, it does not exist to address issues, as they are called, but to upend and subvert that terrestrial abnormality which maims and kills all things and people. Christ did not offer better answers to the social, religious, and political issues of his time or ours. He trampled Death by his death and gave life to those who lay in the tomb, Death being the first-born horror of that abnormality our race chooses every time it gets the chance. There is nothing we do not transmute into life's antithesis—food into weapons, aid into violence, justice into terrorism and war, love into libido, politics into rape, liberation into tyranny, innocence into jaded cynicism. Christian orthodoxy has been around long enough to have learned that all the money, power, and good intentions which systemic abnormality musters can never change this viciousness into virtue, this abnormality into normality. Nor can even Christ's Church accomplish this by its own efforts at alleviating abnormality's pernicious effects or by messages sent to it like telegrams admonishing it to behave. Systemic abnormality, although it does not possess faith's *exousia*, has its own hideous strength, and to underestimate its congenital power for ill is to make certain that it will eat one alive.

Faithful Christian wisdom, flowing straight out from that of Jesus the Christ, has always understood that Christians must hold themselves apart from this systemic abnormality. The Church can cooperate effectively with those afflicted by systemic abnormality only to the extent that they recognize their affliction and are prepared to be helped in withdrawing themselves from its pathology altogether. This is done by recourse to God's grace, by the conversion therapy known as catechesis, and by baptism into Christ's death as condition of what can be nothing less than a new birth. This is a clear and absolutely fundamental paradigm of behavior and attitude regarding how Christians relate to a world in which Death is at home. That many Christians seem to have forgotten this, thinking that it is such a world which establishes and even judges Christian behavior in response to issues such as justice, peace, and life, betrays a modern sort of Pelagianism at work which is made possible by the general demise of baptismal practice and theology in most modern churches. The restoration of such practice and theology as paradigmatic for Christian behavior might suggest that the Church's object of address and endeavor is *not* that world which is the home of systemic abnormality. The Church itself is, rather, the world constantly being conceived under grace and brought to term by faith and death in Christ—a world which is actively cooperating with God in its own rehabilitation. *This* world is not at the periphery of reality but at its center. The shorthand term we use to denote it is Church. It is a City of God in the making. Its antithesis is a City of Man which, by humanity's choice, is a necropolis. For the faithful Christian there can be no choice between the two.

Christians who forget this need reminding that what afflicts the City of Man is not mere mistakes, inadequate policies, or ill-chosen leaders. What afflicts it is nothing less than Death itself, something which this City embraces as its own. Despite rumors to the contrary, this City is not immaculately conceived or without sin. By its own choice it lives a life that is short and brutish because by rejecting communion with its Source it necessarily embraces a Death which is implacably consequent upon its decision to go its own way. It thinks that there might be other options to the Way of Life than the Way of Death. When it discovers otherwise, it twists and turns and dodges, crying foul and oppression and unfair when what it conjures up turns upon it.

This is the enemy which the community of the baptized is bound to subvert and overturn, trampling down its Death by the community's own death accepted freely and celebrated in him who first died such a death for the life of the world. The two premier liturgical endeavors of the Christian community have always been, and remain, baptism and eucharist. Both are about such a death. Both negotiate such a death. From these two all other liturgical endeavors and sacraments proceed. To these two all else returns. By these two all else is framed and the world's malaise is diagnosed, prognosticated, and healed. The assembly of Christian *orthodoxia* exists to die to the world and to itself in Christ according to nothing more or less than the pattern which he himself was constrained to follow. Only thus is Death trampled and does new life flow. Only thus is normality restored.

Having said these things, we may have come about as close to the dark center of the essence of Christian liturgy as words can take us. What we see finally is where the mystery lies, not the mystery itself. The darkness surrounding it is not the murk of chaos and confusion thrown up by a divine Wizard of Oz who needs to hide. The darkness is only the way mortal eyes and minds register a dazzling clarity which is so bright that it overloads creaturely circuits and threatens to burn them out. For as we approach the core of liturgical structures and endeavor, what we encounter there is not data or issues but the Presence of a Holy One who must mask itself in Word and flesh and sacrament and sense out of respect for our weakness if we are to be able to sit at table with it as "friends." Liturgy enables us to regard such a Presence by looking to the right and left of it; to survive its being among us by shielding us from it with the best which creation and human ingenuity can provide; to keep us locked to it by canons of knowledge and behavior which stem from revealed Gospel rather than from human conventions.

Like poetry and art and music, liturgy provides us a means of knowing the kind of thing that can only be known transrationally; that cannot be analyzed, taken apart, spelled out and reassembled. This means of knowing is always a knowledgeable accomplishment which is never stumbled into by accident or mere good intentions. It is worked up into communicable form only by immense intellectual, spiritual, artistic, and even rational effort which must wrestle with the intransigencies of language and things at every point. The outcome is an act of human communication which so drastically affects minds and hearts that reality is perceived in new and unforgettable ways. Lives are changed when Shakespeare talks of brotherhood on St. Crispin's day, when Churchill calls for blood, sweat, and tears in adversity, when Martin Luther King, Jr., tells of his dream, when Bach sets the creed to music, as the inscrutable Holy One enters our midst to dine among friends. Lives are changed because such things change minds, and minds are changed because imaginations are freed by giving human emotions a massive dose of normality. There is nothing easy about this. It takes hard work, suffering, and it costs lives. It is also a risky business because there is no telling where the freed will go. Liberators accomplish only half their task when they liberate. The other half of their labor is to provide a normal place, a free place, on which the liberated may land.

So far as Christian orthodoxy is concerned, this normal place, this free place for the liberated has been chronologically the Sunday, spatially the city. As has been noted already in chapter IV, all the major rites of Christianity evolved from the constantly recurring Sunday worship complexes worked out in the metropolises of the then known world. When the student of liturgy works through the details of developed Christian rites today, he or she must understand that the welter of material being studied is rooted in the ways by which Christians assembled "on the town" to keep the day of the Lord's resurrection, the eighth day of creation, the first day of the new creation and of the world's final era. The agent of this liturgy was not the parish in our modern sense but the local church of the city as a whole, and its full celebration was accomplished not in one service but in many services spanning the whole day. The hymnal of this liturgy was the psalter, its texts almost exclusively scripture, its musical instrument the human voice, its servants the clergy in diversified orders, its president the bishop, its space the city and suburbs, its participants a redeemed and faithful citizenry.

That such a liturgy, which caught and fired the imagination of barbarian peoples, evolved out of previous urban patterns present in the late antique world identifies the way, perhaps, but not the motive which drove Christian worship to take on and renovate such patterns. I suggest that the motive lies in the related matters which have been discussed in this and the preceding three chapters. I also suggest that the free, because normal, place which the liturgy of those days carved out for those to land on whom God's grace and human effort had liberated has shrunk almost to the point of being imperceptible. That liturgy, which had been a sustained transaction with reality restored on a cosmic scale, a transaction played out in an arena suffused with humanity's highest aspirations as well as its most perverse temptations, the city, has become only the thinnest sliver of itself. It is no longer of sufficient robustness to feed the human imagination, much less to motivate Christians in regarding themselves as the world being made new by God in Christ. It has become a narrow place hemmed in by the monstrous structures of state sacrality on one side and bourgeois profanity on the other, a place which attracts few and generates obsessive neuroses even among these. It is no place for the free to cavort in cosmic normality because it is an abnormal place to be. We enter it reluctantly, hanging our redeemed humanity in the vestibule with our coats and taking with us only our reason and printed texts to read as we wile away the time until the seemingly endless and amorphous event of less than an hour is over.

One asks whether this may not be the context responsible for Christians having become so uncreative in art, politics, music, literature and all other forms of endeavor where once they led. It may also be why we never seem to get around to doing much evangelization. We find, when we look into the face of an adult who comes to us from the world of systemic abnormality to ask what we are doing, that we cannot think of much to say. We busy ourselves with picking up and approving fads and programs a decade or two after this world which passes has discarded them and moved on. We risk becoming so uninteresting in the eyes of ourselves and this world that we come to think of ourselves, and to be regarded by this world, as just one more outfit in the standard repertoire of hardly interesting abnormalities; merely another luncheon club for those with ecclesiastical tastes. None shiver when we enter a room. Indeed, few notice.

To point out that one cause contributing to this trend is a reduction of the liturgy similar to reciting the libretto of Mozart's *The Marriage of Figaro* with guitar accompaniment does not usually succeed. To suggest that one way to begin reversing the trend is not to simplify Christian worship further but to enrich and expand it is not often heard with patience. But if liturgy both anchors and frames in normality a life of Christian *orthodoxia*, then restoring liturgy to its appropriate scale is more a requirement than a counsel. The liturgy must be rich and varied because the assembly of faith itself is rich and varied in its nature and operation, that is, catholic in the fullest and most basic sense. Liturgy viewed this way is not only an act; it is an economy and a polity in which baptism and Sunday eucharist hold

172

central place. But these, like the keystone of an arch, function most effectively only in relation to other services and activities which surround and support them. Eucharist is a conjunctive rite in the orthodox assembly's entire life. And keystones without arches, like conjunctions without phrases and sentences, are little more than curiosities. When one goes to Mass, one attends no less only a part of the assembly's Sunday worship than if one attended only morning prayer or baptism or the solemn enrollment of catechumens. When attendance at only one event of the assembly's worship is sanctioned either by law or by custom, no matter how good the intention or valid the secondary theological reasons for such a sanction, the integrity of the whole economy of worship is thrown out of balance and the motive for maintaining the whole economy is weakened. Yet it is precisely the whole economy of Christian worship which is more worthy, or less unworthy, of Christ in his Church and of God's restored world than all good intentions and secondary theological reasons combined. Otherwise cart is put before horse, for good intentions and secondary theological reasons are governed finally by the *lex supplicandi* rather than the other way round.

Yet all this will remain inert unless the principle is restored that Christian life, whatever else it may be, is at root a life of "right worship," a complementary series of acts of supreme normality in which the assembly of faith whole and entire does the world by making a new City. The prevailing understanding of orthodoxy as a set of mind in response to certain propositions, and of the liturgy as an aesthetic or therapeutic endeavor only remotely related to such a mind-set, must be seriously questioned. This will not be easy. The prevailing understanding is affected deeply by perceptions of reality spawned by the secularization process in the West—a process which

Hanna Arendt thinks, as we have noted, threw people not into the world but back upon themselves.[76] This in turn has given rise to a defensive privatism which emphasizes the sovereignty of the individual and regards the world as a stage for masquerade and inauthentic role-playing. Appeals to common good are regarded as oppressive of individual rights. Public style is condemned as elitist. Political categories, such as that of justice, are transmuted into psychological categories upheld by a philosophy of personalism and nurtured on therapeutic techniques. "The society we inhabit today," writes Richard Sennett, "is burdened with the consequences of . . . the effacement of the *res publica* by the belief that social meanings are generated by the feelings of individual human beings."[77] Not only does this belief oversimplify considerably how a continuum of public discourse arises. It also often works to dissolve social bonds in both civil society and Church. Some indeed seem to regard adapting the Church, its worship, and its mission to such an effacement of *res publica* as the most promising way for Church, worship, and mission to survive in a post-Christian world. It is a course of action which pushes the Church into an isolationist position, ghettoizing it in the arena of private and therefore unverifiable feelings and opinions which must be kept out of discussions of public policy, particularly on matters of war and peace and on who possesses social rights and when.

One may doubt that all this will make the world a better place. One is also free to suspect that all this does in fact represent one face of what I have called systemic abnormality, an antisocial malaise which not only disrupts the coherence of the body social but shuts down many of that body's immune systems as well. Given the apparent extent of the malaise, it appears futile to assault it only by words. Its malignancy may be exposed best by placing over against it quite another form of social life which arises from principles which are radically prophetic, evangelical, even exorcistic, and antithetical to the malaise itself. This other form of social life will constitute a form of drastic therapy which cannot be carried on without risk to both patient and therapist, but there seems to be no alternative therapy around. There also seems to be no other therapist so capable of carrying out radical treatment of the malaise as the Church of Jesus Christ. And the liturgical worship of the myriad assemblies which constitute that Church seems to be the most regular, public, and accessible forum in which to prophesy against and then exorcize with the power of God's active Presence this most recent convolution in the world's morbid abnormality.

This means that in a Christian assembly's regular Sunday worship, a restored and recreated world must be so vigorously enfleshed in "civic" form as to give the lie to any antithetical *civitas*—especially to one raised on the slippery footing of Pelagian optimism and the sovereignty of the individual to whom oppression is thought to come only from without. The assembly is not a political party or a special interest group. But it cannot forget that by grace and favor it *is* the world made new; that creation, *not* the state, is a theocracy; and that the freedom with which all people are endowed by the Creator is something which by our own choice is prone to go awry. Along with the blood-bought right of Christian *orthodoxia* to celebrate creation root and branch, there goes an obligation to exorcize continually its human inmates' lust to do their own thing no matter what, especially as doing their own thing blinds them to the risks, duties, and nobility of being creatures of creation's Source and friends of creation's Redeemer.

This is a frightful ministry carried on with trembling hands and a dry mouth, for the world stops being cute

175

when told it is morbid. The Christian assembly is equipped for such a frightful ministry with no more nor less power than that with which Jesus the Christ came to the same ministry in the days of his flesh. It is what his Body corporate is here for. In him, and according to his example and no other, the Christian assembly is obliged to do its best. It was in the doing of his own best that he laid down his life for the life of the world—not in cynical disgust or in limp passivity before the Human Problem, but for love of those who caused the Problem in the first place. His Church can do no less. The Church doing the world as God means it to be done in Christ is the greatest prophecy, the most powerful exorcism, of all.

The Church is seen and felt by all to be doing its best most overtly and accessibly in its steady, regular round of what I have called *orthodoxia*, a life of "right worship" which is one, holy, catholic, and apostolic. It is a life whose enactment is festive, ordered, aesthetic, canonical, eschatological, and normal. The liturgy is nothing more nor less than the Body corporate of Christ Jesus, suffused with his Spirit and assembled in time and place, doing its best by doing the world as the world issues constantly from God's creating and redeeming hand. *What* the liturgical assembly of Christian orthodoxy does is the world. *Where* the liturgical assembly does this is the public forum of the world's radical business, the *Thingplatz* of a restored and redeemed creation. *When* the liturgical assembly does this is the moment of the world's rebirth—the eighth day of creation, the first day of the last and newest age. Nothing less rides upon the act of the assembly, determines its style, lays bare its service and mission for the life of the world.

Conclusion

I have tried during the course of this book to carry on
two related discourses, one on the nature and extent of
Christian liturgy, another on the nature and extent of
liturgical theology strictly so called. I have suggested
that there is an inseparable dialectic between liturgy
and theology which is basic, fundamental, and primary
for the whole of what I have called Christian *orthodoxia*,
a life of "right worship" which quite overflows what
goes on in churches during divine service to permeate
all aspects of a faithful community's daily business. All
these aspects I aggregated under the term "rite" as a
broad designation of the style taken by corporate
Christian life in particular circumstances. I tried to
emphasize that, while liturgy does not exhaust rite, it
does anchor it in the faithful assembly's regular
encounter with the living God in Christ through
worship in Spirit and in truth.

This worship was characterized as festive, ordered,
aesthetic, canonical, eschatological, and above all
normal. Together these characteristics serve to
underline my claim that the liturgical act of Christians
is the primary and irreducible theological act of
Christians; that the two acts are in reality one and the
same act; that this act is communitarian, quotidian,
largely anonymous, possessed of a certain violence,
richly ambiguous, yet neither obscure nor arcane. The
theological dimension of this act is suffused, therefore,
with the same qualities found in the liturgical

dimension of the same act and is done in the first instance by the same people. It is a doing not just of thoughts and ceremonies but of the world itself. Its results quickly escape over the horizons of those who do it. The liturgical scholar tries to account for all this and attempts to help secondary theologians read the process adequately.

I am painfully aware that not all questions have been asked, that by no means all answers have been given. All I have done is to throw open some categories, to erect some schemata in the hope that some parts of both might resonate with the reader's own experience, that initial voice might be given to one or another intuition others may sometimes have had.

I shall be disappointed if anyone has understood me to be dismissing secondary theology, for I am not. I have been seeking its genesis. I shall be disappointed also if anyone has understood me to be advocating emotion over the hard labor of clear thought, for I am not. I have been seeking reconciliation between them. And I shall be most disappointed if anyone has understood me to be extolling a kind of Christian life sunk in a miasma of ritual obsession, for I am not. I have been seeking the place and function of ceremony in human no less than Christian life. I have found it to be both modest and crucial. Christian conversion is not to ecclesiastical tastes but to the Gospel of Jesus Christ become a People.

It is tempting to write off liturgy as nonsense, barbarism, superstition, or adiaphora; to fault it and forget it or to mute its sacrifical core in order to turn it into something benign we can live with easily. Yet liturgy's tombs and crosses, blood and altars, keep us anchored in the brutal reality of who we are and witness to the human city's undiminishable size. We slay each other and erect upon the gory ground not one

Jerusalem but two—in Robert Capon's words, one of despair, another of " . . . a pride of victors feeding on the slain; but leaving the lion as he was before, trapped in ancient reciprocities by which at last all power falls to crows." For all our technologies and liberations, the old order remains unchanged, the deaths of bulls and goats and men achieving nothing.

"Aaron still ineffectual; creation still bloody;
But now haunted by bells within the veil
   where Aaron walks in shadows sprinkling
   blood and bids a new Jerusalem descend.
Endless smoke now rising
Lion become priest
And lamb victim.
The world awaits
The unimaginable union
By which the Lion lifts Himself Lamb slain
And, Priest and Victim,
Brings
The City
Home."[78]

Notes

1. The statement . . . *ut legem credendi lex statuat supplicandi* of Prosper of Aquitaine is cited differently by various authors. This form is in Migne, *Patrologia Latina* vol. 50: col. 555. See P. de Letter, *Prosper of Aquitaine: Defense of St. Augustine*, Ancient Christian Writers 32 (Westminster, Md. 1963).

2. Thomas J. Reece, "A Survey of the American Bishops," *America* 149 (12 November 1983) 285–288, sheds some light on why this is so. One third of the present hierarchy were never pastors at all, and many others only briefly. On the academic side, almost half of them attended only seminaries, and 64 percent possess only an earned B.A. Some 60 percent came to the episcopacy from work in chancery offices.

3. See James Dougherty, *The Fivesquare City: The City in the Religious Imagination* (Notre Dame, Ind. 1980), especially 1–22; Lewis Mumford, *The City in History* (New York 1961); John Baldovin, "The City as Church, the Church as City," *Liturgy: Holy Places* 3:4 (Fall 1983) 69–73.

4. Thus Bernard J. Verkamp, "Recovering a Sense of Sin," *America* 149 (19 November 1983) 305–307.

5. Hannah Arendt, *The Human Condition* (Chicago 1953) 253f.

6. Leonid Ouspensky, *Theology of the Icon* (Crestwood, N.Y. 1978) 224–225.

7. See William Strunk & E.B. White, *The Elements of Style* (New York 1959) 55.

8. J.P. Migne, *Patrologia Latina* vol. 36: cols. 508–509, 510.

9. See Daniel J. Boorstin, *The Discoverers* (New York 1983)

12–19. Also Adolf Adam, *The Liturgical Year* (New York 1979) 35–56; Willi Rordorf, *Sunday* (Philadelphia 1968) passim.

10. For Constantinople see Robert F. Taft, *The Great Entrance* (Rome 1975).

11. See the excellent diagnostic essay of R. Taylor Scott, "The Likelihood of Liturgy," *The Anglican Theological Review* 62 (1982) 103–120. One would not, however, want to accept without reservation some of his suggested remedies.

12. See Richard Krautheimer, *Rome: Profile of a City, 312–1308* (Princeton 1980) 3–58. Also Thomas F. Matthews, *The Early Churches of Constantinople* (University Park, Pa. 1971).

13. A description of such a liturgy during the seventh century can be found in *Ordo Romanus Primus*. See M. Andrieu, *Les Ordines Romani du Haute Moyen Age* (Louvain 1948) vol. 2, 67–108. Also Cuthbert F. Atchley, *Ordo Romanus Primus* (London 1905), an English translation.

14. Urban T. Holmes, "Theology and Religious Renewal," *The Anglican Theological Review* 62 (1980) 19.

15. A random perusal of five academic theological catalogues revealed, for instance, seventeen courses on different "theologies" (systematic, historical, doctrinal, practical, pastoral, liberation, etc.), six courses on "theologies" of this and that, and one course in which "theology" was used adjectivally to modify ethics.

16. Alexander Schmemann, "Theology and Liturgical Tradition," in *Worship in Scripture and Tradition*, ed. Massey Shepherd (Oxford 1963) 175.

17. Massey Shepherd, "The Berakah Award: Response," *Worship* 52 (1978) 312–313.

18. Claude Lévi-Strauss, *Structural Anthropology* (New York 1967) 29–79.

19. Thus Robert F. Taft, "The Structural Analysis of Liturgical Units: An Essay in Methodology," *Worship* 52 (1978) 315. A good example of what Taft is talking about may be seen in his essay, "The Liturgy of the Great Church: An Initial Synthesis of Structure and Interpretation on the Eve of Iconoclasm,"

182

Dumbarton Oaks Papers 34–35 (1982) 45–75. See also his
apologia pro disciplina sua, "Liturgy as Theology," *Worship*
56 (1982) 113–117.

20. See Taft, "The Structural Analysis of Liturgical Units,"
315–317.

21. *Layman's Daily Missal* (Baltimore 1961) 867.

22. Duncan Forrester, in *The Westminster Dictionary of Theology*
(Philadelphia 1983) 421, defines orthodoxy: "The root
meaning is belief in, or assent to, the fundamental truths of
faith." This is certainly not the "root meaning" but a
theologically extended meaning which has come to be layered
over the "root meaning" from the time of the iconoclast
controversy of the eighth century onwards.

23. Thus Geoffrey Wainwright, *Doxology: The Praise of God in
Worship, Doctrine, and Life* (New York 1980) 70. See also David
Power's review in *Worship* 55 (1981) 62–64.

24. David Power, *rev. cit.*, 62.

25. David Power, *rev. cit.*, 64.

26. See Michael Alexander, *The Earliest English Poems* (New
York 1966) 7–22.

27. Boris Pasternak, *Doctor Zhivago*, ch. 14, sec. 8. See
Michael Alexander, *op. cit.*, 18. Also in the translation of Max
Hayward & Manya Harari (Pantheon 1958) 437.

28. Aidan Kavanagh, *Elements of Rite: A Handbook of Liturgical
Style* (New York 1982).

29. See Willi Marxsen, *The Beginnings of Christology*
(Philadelphia 1979).

30. Sermon 340; J. P. Migne, *Patrologia Latina* vol. 38: col.
1483.

31. See William Loerke, "'Real Presence' in Early Christian
Art," in *Monasticism and the Arts*, ed. Timothy Verdon
(Syracuse 1984) 29–51.

32. The move here is from anagogy to exegesis. A sense of
anagogy is captured nicely in an essay reviewing the
intellectual foundations of medieval church building by the

late Summer McK. Crosby, "Abbot Suger's Program for His New Abbey Church," in *Monasticism and the Arts* (Syracuse 1984) 189–206, especially 199 and 203.

33. See *Roles in the Liturgical Assembly* (New York 1981).

34. See S.J.P. van Dijk & J. Hazelden Walker, *The Origins of the Modern Roman Liturgy* (Westminster, Md. 1960).

35. *The Documents of Vatican II*, ed. Walter M. Abbot (New York 1966) 121.

36. Raymond Brown, "'And the Lord Said'? Biblical Reflections on Scripture as the Word of God," *Theological Studies* 42 (1981) 3–19, especially 7.

37. *Art. cit.*, 15.

38. The move here is from a view of liturgy as multivalently *formative* to a view of it as being *didactic*, and it signals a correlative shift away from emphasizing the transaction which is the performance of the liturgy itself to emphasizing the noetic content of what the texts of the liturgy say. Here one might recall the remark of Edward Fisher, *Everybody Steals from God* (Notre Dame, Ind. 1977) 124: "Religious educators need to work harder at communicating the idea that the *way* something is done is at the very foundation of religious life. No activity is religious if it lowers life, and none is secular once it lifts life. *How* a thing is done is rock-bottom communication that goes beyond all words and turns an act into one of worship or into a blasphemy." See also Mark Searle, "Reflections on Liturgical Reform," *Worship* 56 (1982) 426–427.

39. T.S. Eliot, *Four Quartets* (New York 1943) 30.

40. Thus Geoffrey Wainwright, *Doxology* (New York 1980) 21.

41. *Ibid.*

42. *Chapters on Prayer* no. 40, in *Evagrius of Pontus. The Praktikos: Chapters on Prayer*, ed. John Eudes Bamberger (Spencer, Mass. 1970) 66.

43. *Op. cit.*

44. *Op. cit*, 250.

45. See Peter Berger, *The Sacred Canopy* (Garden City, New York 1967).

46. "The Structural Analysis of Liturgical Units," 315f. See above, p. 80–81.

47. *Art. cit.*, 317.

48. *Art. cit.*, 317–318.

49. See Taft, *art. cit.*, 324–329.

50. The sequence can be seen from the earliest times to the present in *Didache* 7–10; Justin's *First Apology* 65; Hippolytus' *Apostolic Tradition* 22:5f.; the *Canons of Hippolytus* 141; and in the *Rite of Christian Initiation of Adults* [1972] no. 232. The text of Hebrews figures prominently in the liturgical commentary by Patriarch Germanus of Constantinople (c. 730) concerning how one is to understand what is about to happen as the eucharistic prayer begins. See Robert F. Taft, "The Liturgy of the Great Church. . .," 56–57.

51. Erving Goffman, *Interaction Ritual: Essays on Face-to-Face Behavior* (New York 1967); *Behavior in Public Places* (New York 1963).

52. See Thomas J. Talley, "A Christian Heortology," *The Times of Celebration*, Concilium Series 142 (New York 1981) 14–21.

53. See Alexander Schmemann, *Introduction to Liturgical Theology* (Portland, Me. 1966), for doctrinal reflections on liturgical order.

54. For example, Josef A. Jungmann, *The Mass of the Roman Rite* (New York 1950) 2 vols.; A. Stenzel, *Die Taufe: eine genetische Erklärung der Taufliturgie* (Innsbruck 1958); Paul F. Bradshaw, *Daily Prayer in the Early Church* (London 1981); Kenneth Stevenson, *Nuptial Blessing: A Study of Christian Marriage Rites* (London 1982).

55. See Kent Bloomer & Charles Moore, *Body, Memory, Architecture* (New Haven 1977) 23–24, 73–74.

56. See J.N.D. Kelly, *Early Christian Creeds* (London 1950).

57. See Gregory Dix, *The Shape of the Liturgy* (London 1945)

18–19, 333f. Also Thomas J. Talley, "History and Eschatology in the Primitive Pascha," *Worship* 47 (1973) 212–221; Robert F. Taft, "Historicism Revisited," *Studia Liturgica* 14 (1982) 97–109.

58. See Ronald L. Grimes, *Beginnings in Ritual Studies* (Washington, D.C. 1982).

59. Thomas Aquinas, *Summa Theologiae* II–II, 1, 2 ad 2.

60. Mary Douglas, *Natural Symbols* (New York 1970) 51–52.

61. See Josef Pieper, *In Tune with the World: A Theory of Festivity* (New York 1965).

62. Pace Arvind Sharma, "Playing Hardball in Religious Studies," *The Council on the Study of Religion Bulletin* 15 (February 1984) 1, 3–4, who seems to confuse first principles such as the existence of Tao or God with matters of a different order, such as the sufficiency of ethics and the fact of whether God actually spoke to Mohammed. While one can never demonstrate a first principle, not everything which cannot be demonstrated is a first principle.

63. I am greatly indebted in what follows to kind suggestions offered me by Eoin de Bhaldraithe, O. Cist., of Bolton Abbey, Kildare, Ireland.

64. *Saint Basil: Ascetical Works*, The Fathers of the Church Series 9 (New York 1950) 364. "Concerning Baptism" is on 339–430.

65. *Ibid.*, passim.

66. See the fine essay of Boniface Ramsey, "Almsgiving in the Latin Church: The Late Fourth and Early Fifth Centuries," *Theological Studies* 43 (1982) 226–259. Basil also notes that the baptized are all expected, no matter what their age, to eat and drink of the eucharist by dominical requirement (John 6:61–70): *loc. cit.*, 386–390.

67. *Loc. cit.*, 364.

68. *Apostolic Tradition* 16:14–18. The ban extends not only to those who engage in violent sports but to those who even attend them as spectators.

69. *Rite of Christian Initiation of Adults* no. 19:2. Also 19:4, where the emphasis on apostolic work and witness is just as strong. In *The Rites of the Catholic Church*, 2nd ed. (New York 1983) 25–26. I comment on this in *The Shape of Baptism* (New York 1978) 131–133.

70. See the Dogmatic Constitution on the Church, *Lumen Gentium* no. 26, in *The Documents of Vatican II*, ed. Walter M. Abbot (New York 1966) 50–51. Also the Constitution on the Sacred Liturgy, *Sacrosanctum Concilium* nos. 41–42; and the 1967 Instruction on Eucharistic Worship, *Eucharisticum Mysterium* no. 7. Both these texts are in *Official Catholic Teachings: Worship and Liturgy*, ed. J. McGivern (Wilmington, N.C. 1978) 210–211, 314 respectively.

71. *Evagrius of Pontus, The Praktikos: Chapters on Prayer*, ed. John Eudes Bamberger (Spencer, Mass. 1970) 14.

72. See my essay, "Eastern Influence on the Rule of St. Benedict," in *Monasticism and the Arts*, ed. Timothy G. Verdon (Syracuse, N.Y. 1984) 53–62.

73. Peter Brown, *The World of Late Antiquity* (London 1971) 102.

74. Rudolf Otto, *The Idea of the Holy*, 2nd ed. (Oxford 1950).

75. Thus Jack S. Boozer, "The Holy," in *The Westminster Dictionary of Christian Theology* (Philadelphia 1983) 261–262.

76. See above, p. 27–28.

77. Richard Sennett, *The Fall of Public Man* (New York 1977) 339. Also Philip Rieff, *The Triumph of the Therapeutic: Uses of Faith after Freud* (New York 1968); James Sallis, "Civility," *America* 150 (3 March 1984) 152–153.

78. Robert F. Capon, *The Supper of the Lamb* (New York 1974) 51–52.

Bibliography

Adam, Adolf, *The Liturgical Year: Its History and Its Meaning after the Reform of the Liturgy*. Pueblo Publishing, New York 1979.

Alexander, Michael, *The Earliest English Poems*. Penguin Books, New York 1966.

Andrieu, M., *Les Ordines Romani du Haute Moyen Age*. Specilegium Sacrum Lovaniense, Louvain 1931–1956, 4 vols.

Arendt, Hannah, *The Human Condition*. University of Chicago Press, Chicago 1953.

Atchley, Cuthbert F., *Ordo Romanus Primus*. A. Moring, London 1905.

Baldovin, John F., "The City as Church, the Church as City," *Liturgy: Holy Places*. Liturgical Conference, Washington D.C. 1983, 69–73.

Basil, Saint, "Concerning Baptism" in *Saint Basil: Ascetical Works*, transl. M. Monica Wagner. The Fathers of the Church Series 9. Fathers of the Church, Inc., New York 1950, 339–430.

Berger, Peter, *The Sacred Canopy*. Doubleday, New York 1967.

Bloomer, Kent C. & Charles W. Moore, *Body, Memory, Architecture*. Yale University Press, New Haven 1977.

Boorstin, Daniel J., *The Discoverers: A History of Man's Search to Know His World and Himself*. Random House, New York 1983.

Boozer, Jack S., "The Holy," *The Westminster Dictionary of Christian Theology*, eds. Alan Richardson & John Bowden. Westminster Press, Philadelphia 1983, 261–262.

Bradshaw, Paul F., *Daily Prayer in the Early Church*. Alcuin Club/SPCK, London 1981.

Brown, Peter, *The World of Late Antiquity*. Thames & Hudson, London 1971.

Brown, Raymond, " 'And the Lord Said'? Biblical Reflections on Scripture as the Word of God," *Theological Studies* 42 (1981) 3–19.

Capon, Robert F., *The Supper of the Lamb*. Doubleday Image Books, New York 1974.

Crosby, Sumner McK., "Abbot Suger's Program for His New Abbey Church," in *Monasticism and the Arts*, ed., Timothy Verdon. Syracuse University Press, Syracuse, New York 1984, 189–206.

Dix, Gregory, *The Shape of the Liturgy*. Dacre Press, London 1945.

The Documents of Vatican II, ed. Walter M. Abbot. America Press, New York 1966.

Dougherty, James, *The Fivesquare City: The City in the Religious Imagination*. University of Notre Dame Press, Notre Dame, Ind. 1980.

Douglas, Mary, *Natural Symbols: Explorations in Cosmology*. Pantheon, New York 1970.

Eliot, T.S., *Four Quartets*. Harcourt, Brace & World, New York 1943.

Evagrius of Pontus, *The Praktikos: Chapters on Prayer*, ed. John Eudes Bamberger. Cistercian Publications, Spencer, Mass. 1970.

Fisher, Edward, *Everybody Steals from God*. University of Notre Dame Press, Notre Dame, Ind. 1977.

Forrester, Duncan, "Orthodoxy," *The Westminster Dictionary of Theology*, eds. Alan Richardson & John Bowden. Westminster Press, Philadelphia 1983, 421–422.

Goffman, Erving, *Behavior in Public Places: Notes on the Social Organization of Gatherings*. Free Press, New York 1963.

190

Goffman, Erving, *Interaction Ritual: Essays on Face-to-Face Behavior*. Doubleday Anchor Books, Garden City, N.Y. 1967.

Grimes, Ronald L., *Beginnings in Ritual Studies*. University Press of America, Washington, D.C. 1982.

Holmes, Urban T., "Theology and Religious Renewal," The *Anglican Theological Review* 62 (1980) 3–19.

Jungmann, Josef A., *The Mass of the Roman Rite*. Benziger Brothers, New York 1950, 2 vols.

Kavanagh, Aidan, "Eastern Influences on the Rule of St. Benedict," *Monasticism and the Arts*, ed. Timothy G. Verdon. Syracuse University Press, Syracuse, N.Y. 1984, 53–62.

Kavanagh, Aidan, *Elements of Rite: A Handbook of Liturgical Style*. Pueblo Publishing, New York 1982.

Kavanagh, Aidan, *The Shape of Baptism: The Rite of Christian Initiation*. Pueblo Publishing, New York 1978.

Kelly, J.N.D., *Early Christian Creeds*. Longmans, Green, London 1950.

Krautheimer, Richard, *Rome: Profile of a City, 312–1308*. Princeton University Press, Princeton, N.J. 1980.

Layman's Daily Missal. Helicon Press, Baltimore 1961.

Lévi-Strauss, Claude, *Structural Anthropology* (1958). Anchor Books, New York 1967.

Loerke, William, " 'Real Presence' in Early Christian Art," in *Monasticism and the Arts*, ed. Timothy Verdon. Syracuse University Press, Syracuse, N.Y. 1984, 29–51.

Marxsen, Willi, *The Beginnings of Christology*. Fortress Press, Philadelphia 1979.

Mathews, Thomas F., *The Early Churches of Constantinople: Architecture and Liturgy*. Pennsylvania State University Press, University Park 1971.

Migne, J.P., *Patrologiae Cursus Completus, Series Latina*. Paris 1844–1890, suppl. 1958–1974. 221 vols.

Mumford, Lewis, *The City in History*. Harcourt, Brace, Jovanovich, New York 1961.

Official Catholic Teachings: Worship and Liturgy, ed. J. McGivern. Consortium–McGrath, Wilmington, N.C. 1978.

Otto, Rudolf, *The Idea of the Holy: An Inquiry into the Non-Rational Factor in the Idea of the Divine and Its Relation to the Rational*, 2nd ed. Oxford University Press, Oxford 1950.

Ouspensky, Leonid, *Theology of the Icon*. St. Vladimir's Press, Crestwood, N.Y. 1978.

Pasternak, Boris, *Doctor Zhivago*, transl. Max Hayward & Manya Harari. Pantheon, New York 1958.

Pieper, Josef, *In Tune With the World: A Theory of Festivity*. Harcourt Brace & World, New York 1965.

Power, David, "Review of *Doxology. The Praise of God in Worship, Doctrine, and Life* by Geoffrey Wainwright," *Worship* 55(1981) 62–64.

Ramsey, Boniface, "Almsgiving in the Latin Church: The Late Fourth and Early Fifth Centuries," *Theological Studies* 43(1982) 226–259.

Reece, Thomas J., "A Survey of the American Bishops," *America* 149 (12 November 1983) 285–288.

Rieff, Philip, *The Triumph of the Therapeutic: Uses of Faith after Freud*. Harper & Row, New York 1968.

The Rites of the Catholic Church, 2nd ed. Pueblo Publishing, New York 1983.

Roles in the Liturgical Assembly [the twenty-third Liturgical Conference of Saint Serge 1977], Pueblo Publishing, New York 1981.

Rordorf, Willi, *Sunday: The History of the Day of Rest and Worship in the Earliest Centuries of the Christian Church*. Westminster Press, Philadelphia 1968.

Sallis, James, "Civility," *America* 150(3 March 1984) 152–153.

Schmemann, Alexander, *Introduction to Liturgical Theology*. American Orthodox Press, Portland, Me. 1966.

Schmemann, Alexander, "Theology and Liturgical

Tradition," in *Worship in Scripture and Tradition*, ed. Massey Shepherd. Oxford University Press, Oxford 1963, 165–178.

Scott, R. Taylor, "The Likelihood of Liturgy," *The Anglican Theological Review* 62(1982) 103–120.

Searle, Mark, "Reflections on Liturgical Reform," *Worship* 56(1982) 411–430.

Sennett, Richard, *The Fall of Public Man*. Knopf, New York 1977.

Sharma, Arvind, "Playing Hardball in Religious Studies," *The Council on the Study of Religion Bulletin* 15(February 1984) 1, 3–4.

Shepherd, Massey, "The Berakah Award: Response," *Worship* 52(1978) 299–313.

Stenzel, Alois, *Die Taufe: eine genetische Erklärung der Taufliturgie*. Felizian Rauch, Innsbruck 1958.

Stevenson, Kenneth, *Nuptial Blessing: A Study of Christian Marriage Rites*. Alcuin Club/SPCK, London 1982.

Strunk, William, & E.B. White, *The Elements of Style*. Macmillan, New York 1958.

Taft, Robert F., *The Great Entrance: A History of the Transfer of Gifts and Other Pre-Anaphoral Rites of the Liturgy of St. John Chrysostom*. Pontifical Oriental Institute, Rome 1975.

Taft, Robert F., "Historicism Revisited," *Studia Liturgica* 14(1982) 97–109.

Taft, Robert F., "Liturgy as Theology," *Worship* 56(1982) 113–117.

Taft, Robert F., "The Liturgy of the Great Church: An Initial Synthesis of Structure and Interpretation on the Eve of Iconoclasm," *Dumbarton Oaks Papers* 34–35(1982) 45–75.

Taft, Robert F., "The Structural Analysis of Liturgical Units: An Essay in Methodology," *Worship* 52(1978) 314–329.

Talley, Thomas J., "A Christian Heortology," *The Times of Celebration*, Concilium Series 142, ed. David Power. Seabury Press, New York 1981, 14–21.

Talley, Thomas, J., "History and Eschatology in the Primitive Pascha," *Worship* 47(1973) 212–221.

Van Dijk, S.J.P., & J. Hazelden Walker, *The Origins of the Modern Roman Liturgy: The Liturgy of the Papal Court and the Franciscan Order in the Thirteenth Century.* Newman Press, Westminster, Md. 1960.

Verkamp, Bernard J., "Recovering a Sense of Sin," *America* 149(19 November 1983) 305–307.

Wainwright, Geoffrey, *Doxology: The Praise of God in Worship, Doctrine, and Life.* Oxford University Press, New York 1980.

Index

Lord's Day *(kyriake)*, 56

Lucernarium, 60

Luther, Martin, 12

M

Magisterium, 115–116

Marriage, 110

Marriage of Figaro, 172

Marx, Karl, 26, 27

McGivern, J., 187 n. 70

Michelangelo, 24

Ministry, 78, 82

Missa, 58

Monasticism, 6

Monica, Saint, 99

Moon, Reverend, 5

Moses, 24, 25, 75, 92, 125

Mozart, W.A., 172

N

Niebuhr, Richard, 50

Nietzsche, Friedrich, 26

Newton, Isaac, 12

North American Academy of Liturgy, 78–79

Nuclear war, American bishop's pastoral on, 158

O

Ordo Romanus I, 106–107

Oriental Orthodox Church of Ethiopia, 132

Origen, 18

Otto, Rudolf, 164, 187 n.74

Ouspensky, Leonid, 41, 181 n.6

Theologia prima, 74ff., 77, 78, 83. *See also* Theology, primary

Theologia secunda, 74ff., 77, 78. *See also* Theology, secondary

Theologians, as pastors, 17–19

Theology
as aboriginally liturgical, 74ff., 89
as academic endeavor, 17, 18, 19
and Bible, 19, 20
as communitarian in genesis, 74f.
and Eastern Christianity, 124
and faith, 4, 18, 67, 147
liturgical, 75–95, 135, 138, 143f., 152–154
ontological condition of, 75
and the pastoral task, 17–19, 20
patristic, 18
primary, (theologia prima, q.v.), 89, 96, 109, 110, 124, 146, 151
as religious discourse, 73
secondary, (theologia secunda, q.v.), 78, 88, 90, 95, 96, 100,
    103, 109, 110, 118, 124, 127–128, 131–133, 146, 151, 173, 178
sources of, 7–8, 69
as sustained dialectic, 76
systematic, 19 n.124, 143, 145f., 146, 152. *See also* Liturgy

Thomas Aquinas, Saint, 11, 16, 51, 52, 186 n.59

Trent, Council of, 81, 108

Truth, scientific, 9

U

Unitarians, 5

Utopia, 25

V

Vespers, 57, 60

Vestments, 110

W

Wagner, Richard, 63

Wainwright, Geoffrey, 123ff., 183 n.23, 184 nn.40,41, 185 nn.46,47,48,49

Weber, Max, 27

Whitman, Walt, 48, 49

Wilde, Oscar, 26

Wisdom, 26, 167

World, 4, 7, 8, 11, 14, 19, 21, 23, 29, 34–36, 37, 38, 39, 42–44, 45, 52, 55, 135, 141, 168, 176. *See also* Church

Worship, 4, 8, 21–22, 60, 63, 76, 83, 87, 91, 92, 96, 97–98, 99, 100, 101, 106, 109, 113, 117, 123, 124–125, 127, 132, 133, 134, 136, 140–141, 147, 152, 165, 176. *See also* Church